Ponder on It, Pilgrims

The Bucolic Mark Twain on Critter Councils,
Cookie Bandits, and Texas Grit

By Charles Hamm

DEDICATION

This book is dedicated to Kathy, Steven, Staci, Robyn, Sophie, Gracie, Olivia, Lillie, Kolton, Sallie, Lucas, Scott, and Ed. Also, to the wonderful followers on LinkedIn who encouraged me to write it, Mr. Philip Reed, who would not take no for an answer, and Ms. Hilary, who made it all possible.

GET IN TOUCH WITH CHARLES

To learn more about Charles and what he's up to on Round Mountain, visit CharlesHamm.com.

TABLE OF CONTENTS

"AT THE END OF THE DAY, THERE IS NOTHING LIKE
GETTING BACK TO THE CABIN,
SITTING DOWN, AND WATCHING THE FIRE.
IT QUIETS THE MIND AND SOOTHES THE SOUL.
WE ALL NEED TO FIND SUCH TIMES IN OUR LIVES."

~CHARLES HAMM

FOREWORD

That was the thought running through my head when I met Charles Hamm.

We've all experienced a moment of meeting someone who we knew was special, who we will never forget. Charles gifted me that moment, and I am sure after you read his book, the magnum opus of his life, you will feel the same.

Charles is the common sense we are all missing in this upside-down world. He is the soothing voice that we all long to hear when a more experienced adult takes charge. He is the sigh of relief we feel when we slow down and pay attention. At a time when we are all striving for "wisdom, right now, please," he brings it to you. I like to think we can borrow the knowledge he has gathered from his years on Earth to make our lives a little more comfortable and less worrisome.

We are all questing for permission to slow down, to have real conversations, to speak up, to be heard, to live as we want. Even in this world of you can "have it your way," it doesn't feel like that.

It feels like a bunch of noise.

Charles is the quiet barometer we have all been straining to reach.

His stories invite and encourage you to sit a spell. To ponder on your own life, on what has brought you to where you are today.

His voice is one of the reasons people flock to him. His unabashed pride in his country and state ("Texas is like another country," he says), his joy at being a grandfather to seven cookie bandits, and his affection for his Round Mountain Critter Council members: Thelma, the doe-eyed matriarch, Spuds, who leads from the rear, Rex, a nimble coyote with his nose to ground and Rocko, a direct descendant of Davy Crockett's coonskin cap is unmatched. The way he spins his yarns is a testament to turning the world around you into what you want it to be.

One of wonder.

One of might.

One of imagination.

One of delight.

Charles exercises the power we all still have that we forget about. The ability to change how we perceive the world.

In the months I have known Charles, that is what he has brought to me and to his adoring audience, who huddle around him as the patriarch of the campfire.

When we were bandying about titles for this book, Charles and I talked about people noting that he was a Mark Twain reincarnation. Twain was a masterful storyteller of transportive qualities. He possessed a magic to pick you up and plunk you into a world he had a heavy hand in making, but he permitted freedom as well. To insert yourself into the scenery and belong. To be accepted in a world that finds you good enough and wants you there. You met people you swore you had known a thousand years. They brought with them stories as old as the mountain.

Salt-of-the-Earth stories, stories explaining fundamental truths, irrevocable events in one's life. This is where we are. On the bedrock of the mountain where the stories grow and take you out of your life and into another existence, where it feels like more is possible. Where the person you want to be is possible. What a special invitation to be beckoned up onto that porch to be entertained as you wonder, "Is that really whiskey in that mug?" Once there, your only job is to listen.

After the book was mostly put together and I was still starry-eyed over its content, Charles introduced The Four Golden Questions, which take into account how a wise man thinks, speaks, what he does, and what he feels. I love books like that. They make us grow. It is why we must carve out time to get lost in them.

How often do you give yourself the gift of time to try and answer what a wise man would do? What he would say, how he would feel and think? If you're antsy reading about taking the time to assess such a wise man, then you need to do this more than you realize. But we don't, do we? We make excuses to stop thinking deeply. We make excuses to rush through life, all the while proclaiming our busy-ness, yet knowing we choose where we spend our time. Sometimes, loving that we have these "reasons" to avoid our true emotions even as we wish harder for life to slow down.

We are perpetually searching for balance.

I know you want to have a reason to sink into that uncommon book that will slow the clock.

This book is that reason.

Now, make a promise to yourself to leave your world behind for the time it takes you to read it. Turn off your phone, all those incessant pings and dings we hear an astounding number of times a day. Slide down in your chair, take off your shoes. Then step into mountain country. Inhale the crisp, unpolluted air, feel the soft grass between your toes as you scrunch up your face into a smile, spying Thelma and the fawn twins, a whispery red fox slipping through the forest, scampering bear cubs, and the rest of the mountain menagerie.

When you emerge, hand this wisdom off to someone else who you think needs it, but keep a little for yourself. For another day, and another time when you can't resist climbing that mountain and swapping your world for one that you can access anytime simply by closing your eyes and believing you are there.

Enjoy yourself.

Charles will greet you on the other side of the mountain. Just follow the scent of his tobacco pipe, the fresh pine encircling his cozy cabin, and of course, the home-baked cookies, and you're there.

With gratitude,
Hilary Jastram
Founder, J. Hill Creative | Bookmark Publishing House

P.S. This book has been arranged to share specific sentiments in certain sections, and throughout it, you will see quotes from famous people and quotes without an author listed. Those are the ones Charles himself has dreamed up—Texas Grit, as he calls them—and, in no particular order, they are sprinkled throughout this book to improve your experience and allow you to pause and reflect.

My favorite Texas Grit saying is:

"FOLLOW THE WAY OF PEACE AND CRITTERS."

INTRODUCTION

Listen up, you magnificent sons and daughters of mothers.

I'm fixin' to tell you a bit about this book. Now, I know what y'all are thinkin'. *What would some old geezer, who roams about in backwoods east Texas, consortin' with a bunch of wild critters, have to say about anything? Why would he be writin' a book?*

Well, fact is, I got horsed into it by a bunch of pilgrims on LinkedIn who took to followin' me around.

Since I wrote the dang thing, I 'spose you deserve an explanation of what you're about to git into. So gather around, boys and girls, and let me tell ya a story.

Once upon a time, I was sittin' in my rockin' chair on the front porch of my little cabin, rockin' a bit. It was early mornin', a bit of a chill was in the air, and all my critters were comin' up to Round Mountain to git their belly rubs.

It's a tradition, you see.

After the belly rubbin' was all done, and my critters scattered about to git their day started, I took to rockin' once more and doin' some ponderin'. That day, I wrote down my mornin' musing and posted it on LinkedIn.

I had no idea what to expect and didn't give it much thought. Figured it might even go nowhere, but that was no skin off my nose. I had a fresh cigar, comfy boots, and a beautiful day to keep me occupied.

Well, a bunch of pilgrims read it, seemed to like it, and wrote some nice comments.

So, I did some more rockin', and ponderin', and wrote another post. Same dang thang. Lots of responses.

In hindsight, I should have stopped right there. But I kept on rockin', ponderin', and writin'. Next thang I know, these LinkedIn folks wanted me to write a book. I played them off the best I could. *Shucks*, I thought, *that sounds like a lot of trouble. I'm no book writer.*

But I am a book reader. When I sit down, ready to read, I make sure my book has no agenda. Instead, I prepare to stretch my mind to take in new knowledge that will make me think differently, add to what I already know, or take away what I think I know.

Then every once in a while, there comes a day when I prepare to flip through some fresh pages, and the more I read, the more my mind is *smoked*. On those days, I can't help but think, *how come I'm just hearin' about this guy or gal? They wrote this book twenty years ago! Where have I been?*

I kept doin' my thang, rockin', ponderin', writin', and of course, readin' the books that held my interest. Before I knew it, years went by.

Then one day, this LinkedIn feller set in on me and just wouldn't take no for an answer about writin' it all down. He even got me hooked up with this lady from someplace up north of here, called Minnesota.

Her name is Ms. Hilary Jastram, and she is a publisher. We talked, and she charmed the socks off of me. She is a great professional in the publishing world, a delightful lady, and a joy to work with. Truth be told, I think she horsed me, too!

Next thang I know, I'm writin' this here book. Now, I just wrote it. Ms. Hilary made it a book. She deserves all the credit for what you are holding in your hands right now.

This book's about learning to roll with the punches of life. It's about horse sense, common sense, and living wisely. Lots of folks are smart these days, but it doesn't follow that being smart will make you wise. Wisdom is the key to living in the context of a chaotic, angry world and being content regardless of circumstances.

It's about keeping your head screwed on straight and giving good advice to those who will listen. It's about self-discipline, self-control, and taking charge of your life.

I wrote it to give you the ability to be calm when everyone else seems to be going bat poop crazy.

The concept I kept coming back to was wisdom. It seems to be a concept from another time. When was the last time you heard someone referred to as "wise?" I'm guessing it's been a long time.

I hope this book heralds the beginning of a "Wisdom Revolution," where people will be nice to each other, respectful of others, and find inner peace with themselves as well as their fellow man.

This is the better way.

I tried my best to create a book you will appreciate, and that might cause you to think a little differently from the moment you pick it up.

One of the most important sections of the book is the Four Golden Questions. They're comin' right up after this piece. The entire book that follows is directly or indirectly based on living your life by coming back to these questions. What would a wise person do? What would a wise person say? What would a wise person think? What would a wise person feel? The answer to each question will always be a choice. I have learned that the twists and turns of life always come back to individual choices; that's why I include this bit.

In the coming pages, you'll also find a lot of my life's stories, learn about the people who shaped my life, my ponderins', and good ol' Texas Grit.

I'm now seventy-five years old, as I write, closing in on seventy-six, hard and fast. I've had a long life with every sort of personal experience and time to observe the good and bad of myself and other folks.

Regardless of what I've learned, I've always tried to learn the lessons of foolishness, so I can avoid them—even as I've known great sorrow, intense grief, and the cruel consequences of life and death.

My adult life began in the United States Marine Corps. I was nineteen years old. I'm a Vietnam veteran, and after four years of service, received an honorable discharge with the rank of E-5 sergeant. In so many ways, this time in my life molded and shaped me into the man I am now.

I went to college on the GI bill and got a BA degree, majoring in Classical Greek and Hebrew. I married, raised three great kids, and now have seven little cookie bandits who are the joy of my life.

I have started several businesses along the way. Some failed, and others were successful. I worked hard and didn't retire until I was seventy-four. But, through it all, I learned about life, what's really important, and how to choose to be happy.

At best, I now define myself as an old man struggling not to be an old fool. Living wisely is a daily struggle. You don't just become wise. With every decision in the course of a day, we must make a choice. Being foolish is usually the easier way. Of course, it appeals to our baser nature. But making wise choices elevates us as human beings and connects us to our higher, spiritual nature.

When it comes to my LinkedIn followers, I often ask myself, *who are these wonderful people who are so nice to me?*

Without them, this book wouldn't be a reality, but now I'm glad I wrote it. It is my sincere prayer that people of all ages and walks of life read it and benefit from it. I wish, especially, that young folks read it, so they can make wise decisions at a time in their lives when major decisions must be made with lifelong consequences—for good or ill.

This book has been my destiny. Maybe it's the reason to have lived and endured. I have struggled through the years, wondering why I survived events that some didn't. Stuck on *what is the meaning of it all?* Now, as an old man, all the stars seemed to have aligned, and people have come into my life out of nowhere, encouraging me to write. So here we are.

I've shared some of my deepest secrets and laid bare my soul. It was painful at times, but amazing people stood with me, and through the process, some old wounds have healed. I've found writing to be therapeutic. I hope my words will enrich your life and encourage you to ponder on what needs healing in you.

You are always welcome on the mountain and on my LinkedIn page at: https://bit.ly/CharlesHamm. Or you can find me on my website at: CharlesHamm.com.

Now git to readin', and ponder on it, pilgrims. I'll see you on the inside.

THE FOUR GOLDEN QUESTIONS

Each day of our lives, we are faced with four constants that demand wise decisions if we are to live up to our potential.

They are things we do, things we say, things we think, and things we feel.

Here are the four golden questions you should constantly ask yourself. They are the keys to making wise decisions, taking control of your life, and living happy and well. Consider how you would answer them as you read through this book to give yourself the most insightful experience.

1. What would a wise person do?

2. What would a wise person say?

3. What would a wise person think?

4. What would a wise person feel?

1. What Would a Wise Person Do?

When you try to answer this question, it's paramount to realize you need to take some action or make a decision. That could be anything. But remember, what you do will often not just affect you, but it will affect the lives of other people. The answer to this question might often be doing nothing at all.

2. What Would a Wise Person Say?

Words are powerful, and once said, cannot be unsaid. What you say is often in response to what someone has said to you. Choose your words wisely. Again, often the best thing to say is nothing.

3. What Would a Wise Person Think?

You have control over your thoughts and can learn a lot about yourself by taking note of what captures your mind.

Do you mostly dwell on the negative and destructive, or do you think about positive, uplifting, and peaceful thoughts?

4. What Would a Wise Person Feel?

What you feel is a reflection of your heart.

Is your heart filled with darkness or light?

Will you find hate, unforgiveness, jealousy, and misery in your heart?

Or will you find love, forgiveness, happiness, and joy?

This, too, is a choice.

Every day, the four golden questions play out in real life.

It is my hope through sharing my life and perspective that if you are struggling, your life can get better because of the way you choose to answer these questions.

GRIN LIKE A POSSUM EATIN' A SWEET TATER

"Happiness"

GRANDPA'S GIFT

"We all have our 'good old days' tucked away inside our hearts, and we return to them in daydreams like cats to favorite armchairs." - Unknown

I awakened to the crow of a rooster.

In that first moment of consciousness, I wasn't sure where I was.

All of us have had that feeling of not waking up in our own beds. I was in a feather bed, a mattress filled with chicken feathers, and my own feather pillow. I loved it, and I loved where I quickly realized I was.

I was at Grandma and Grandpa's house in rural Nicholas County, Kentucky. I smiled one of those deep smiles that come to us when we are totally content and happy, just embracing the moment. It was a feeling that nothing could be any better than this.

THIS TWINKLING IN TIME WAS SEVENTY-ONE YEARS AGO AS I WRITE THIS. IT WAS 1950, TO BE EXACT, AND I WAS A FOUR-YEAR-OLD LITTLE BOY, INNOCENT TO A FAULT.

Grandma and Grandpa had a small four-room house with a back porch. I didn't fully appreciate it at the time, but it was truly a special place. My daddy was born there, as was my grandpa. My great-grandpa, a Confederate Civil War veteran, had built it when he came home from the war and had died here. Great-grandpa had also built the root cellar just outside the back door, and it is still there to this day.

I visited the old home place just last year with my son, Steven. As always, we both stood in reverential awe.

THIS IS HALLOWED GROUND IN OUR FAMILY HISTORY.

Below is the only picture I have of the home place. That is me standing on the front porch, barely visible, with grandpa's dog, Mac, eager to go play.

I could tell by the morning sounds of the house that grandma was up. The smell of something being prepared for breakfast made my mouth water. I was hoping for pancakes with bacon or fried bologna.

**NOBODY EVER LIVED WHO
COULD COOK LIKE GRANDMA.**

This picture gives you a better idea of what Grandma's stove looked like. I can still smell her pancakes!

She had an old wood-burning cooking stove, and she worked wonders with it. She would start a fire in the fire chamber on the left side of the stove and let it burn until the top of the stove was the right heat. Grandma was a master. The pancake batter was made from scratch, and she made her own syrup by boiling water, adding the right amount of sugar, and letting it cook down until it was just right.

I dressed and hurried to the back of the house to the room where the table was. Grandpa was sitting there drinking coffee. I looked into the next room, and there was grandma busy fixing breakfast. *YES!! Pancakes and bacon. What a day this is going to be.*

After we had finished breakfast, Grandpa looked at me and said, "Let's go feed the hogs." His voice was firm. Grandpa didn't ever ask me anything. He told me.

He'd never ask, "Would you like to go with me to feed the hogs?" No, it was, "Let's go feed the hogs." No option was implied. That was Grandpa's way. I liked it.

He talked to me like a man. Sure, he was a might gruff on the surface, but I could see the kind, loving man inside Grandpa even then. Fact is, I couldn't wait to go help him with the morning chores.

Grandpa and I left the house, went through the gate, and closed it behind us. We set out for the corn crib, walking in silence. Suddenly Grandpa stopped. He pointed at me and commanded, "Pull my finger." Without thought or hesitation, I obediently reached out, wrapped my little hand around his extended finger, and gave it a tug.

Grandpa tooted.

THERE ARE NO WORDS TO ADEQUATELY DESCRIBE MY RESPONSE. I STRUGGLE TO CONVEY THAT MOMENT AS I WRITE THIS PARAGRAPH. TO SAY I LAUGHED ISN'T ENOUGH. I BECAME HYSTERICAL.

I wish there was an even more descriptive word than this. I lost complete control of myself. Grandpa walked on as if nothing had happened. I tried to follow, but I was laughing so hard my legs failed me. I staggered about. I bent over with laughter. I fell facedown onto the ground and rolled onto my back. My legs spasmed, and my heels kicked against the Earth. My entire body, soul, and spirit were possessed. I howled. I guffawed. I held my stomach with my hands. My sides ached. It was hard to breathe. I couldn't stop laughing or regain control of myself.

Grandpa's gift was a memory. Before or since, I have not laughed with such total, unrestrained abandon and lack of dignity.

To this day, seventy-one years later, I cannot tell this story without literally laughing out loud. I'm laughing as I write. It was the funniest thing that ever happened to me.

WHAT A PRICELESS GIFT TO GIVE A LITTLE BOY.

When God wired our minds, he gave us the gift of long-term memory. These memories, however, can certainly be a two-edged sword. We all have good memories as well as bad ones. Good memories stand by themselves and are cherished. Bad memories should also be embraced. If taken as they should be, they will not haunt a wise man. They serve him life lessons to be learned. They are a treasure trove of wisdom to the wise. I have only in recent years come to fully understand this.

Grandpa gave me one more memory that was the antithesis of the day in the barnyard. It happened on the day he died five years later, when I was nine years old.

Grandpa's death was my first experience with death.

He died as he had lived, courageous, with his boots on and a strong sense of right and wrong. He was a man who took care of his business, a man who would stand his ground. When he died, he got more press than a simple obituary in the *Carlisle Mercury*, the newspaper published in the small town of Carlisle, Kentucky.

GRANDPA MADE THE NEWS.

Grandpa went fishing one day, and when he came back up to his truck, someone had stolen his tools. He thought he knew who had taken them, and since he knew where the man lived, he drove up to his house. Grandpa got out of his truck, skipped going to the front door, and walked straight into a small shed—where he found his tools. While carrying them out to his truck, a young man known to have mental problems came out of the house with a rifle. Grandpa fought with the man for the gun, and as they struggled, the man broke free and fired, killing Grandpa.

The man was charged with murder but was found to be mentally ill. He was committed to a mental institution.

I will share more about Grandpa's last moment on this Earth in a coming chapter, in case you want a few more details. I did.

Grandpa's last gift to me was a memory of intense grief, a memory of lessons I had to learn. Over time, I've come to cherish both.

I often tell people, "Make a memory." Is there any greater gift? Is there any greater legacy than to do that?

Ponder on it, pilgrims.

Own Yourself

If someone treats you like a rented mule,
keep them at a distance.
Ride with folks who make you grin.

WHAT A RIDE!

"If there is any immortality to be had among us human beings, it is certainly only in the love that we leave behind. Fathers like mine don't ever die."
~Leo Buscaglia

Mom was cooking supper when Daddy got home.

She heard him pull up in the driveway. He came in the back door, took off his boots, and walked into the kitchen. He kissed her on the cheek, and since she was still working on supper, he could tell it would be a bit before it would be ready.

He walked into the living room, sat down in his recliner, kicked back, and turned on the TV. Whatever was on the TV might've been the last thing on Daddy's mind at that time. As he sat there, he had lived seventy-two years, eight months, and ten days.

Mom called him about ten minutes later: "Supper is ready."

He didn't come.

She called again, a little louder, thinking he had not heard her.

He didn't come.

SHE WALKED INTO THE LIVING ROOM AND SAID, "SUPPER IS REA—"

THE LAST WORD HUNG ON HER LIPS.

Daddy was dead. He had died instantly from a massive heart attack without so much as a sound.

As I marked my last birthday, declaring myself three-quarters of a century old, my mind wandered off into a number of directions.

Memories flooded me of times gone by. Times of life, death, joy, sorrow, and grief. I thought of the ebbs and flows of my life, the good times and bad. I pondered the march of the years and its cycles.

Heck, I used to be a little boy, but time had changed all that. Now I often sit on the cabin porch, a man deep into the winter of my life, rockin' and doin' some thinkin'.

The men in my family often die instantly from a heart attack. It must be in the genes. I have already lived longer than most of them and have thought for years this could be my fate as well. I really didn't expect to live as long as I have.

When I "retired," I had plans to do some traveling. There are places the world over that I would like to see. Most of them are archeological sites of great antiquity.

But my plans were put on hold because of the Covid-19 virus. I won't get started on what I think about that, but it did restrict my ability to travel as I would have wished.

I have no idea how much longer I'll live, but I've been feeling a mild sense of regret that I have not seen some of these places. Traveling is at the top of my bucket list. I think as I rock, *how much time do I have left?* And then, *does it really matter?*

On the other hand, I have done some traveling, having been on an incredible journey for over seventy-five years now.

The heck of it is that all of us have, but most of us have failed to notice for the most part. We have sat back as we traveled along; we have not been looking out the window as the most phenomenal sites imaginable passed before our eyes.

WE ARE ALL SPACE TRAVELERS. WE SIT ON THIS TINY SPACECRAFT WE CALL EARTH AND ARE TAKING QUITE A RIDE.

Every one of us is spinning about 1,000 miles an hour, and we have divided this movement into twenty-four equal measures of time, which is how we get those hours in the first place.

This is how we mark one complete revolution of the Earth's spin cycle. We call twenty-four hours one day as marked by the position of the Sun in the sky at its zenith—noon. In the course of a day, as the Earth spins, we have a period of daylight and darkness. On the day of the equinoxes, the day and night are equal and last twelve hours each.

But we aren't just spinning. We're movin', and I mean really movin'. The Earth is going eighteen miles per second, or about 67,000 miles per hour, and circling the Sun. That is about 1,608,000 miles a day and 584,000,000 miles to complete one revolution around the Sun—or a year. We mark the completion of one orbit by the equinoxes: either the first day of spring or the first day of fall, at the instant the Sun "crosses" the equator. Now, don't forget, we're ridin' on this thang and see the wonders of the changing sky along the way.

Hold on! I'm just getting started.

The Earth doesn't sit up straight. It is tilted over, right now, to about 23.4 degrees; this is what causes the seasons of the year as we move around the Sun. No matter if it's spring, summer, fall, or winter, it's rockin' back and forth, going from 22.1 degrees to 24.5 degrees. It completes this cycle in about 41,000 years.

There are actually three different ways that the Earth is moving. It is spinning, moving around the Sun, and it is rocking. The spinning cycle is the most obvious. It is easy to observe as it orbits around the Sun. I suppose most people are aware of this. However, the current state of our educational system leaves me to ponder how many people on the street are aware of the tilt and rocking motion of the Earth.

We have to consider that the Sun is *also* traveling through space at about 124 miles a second, or about 448,000 miles an hour. The Sun orbits our galaxy, the Milky Way, every 225 to 250 million years. Since the Earth is traveling along with it, this becomes an additional part of our trip—what I call the Earth's fourth movement.

Now, you might be doin' a little ponderin' yourself, thinkin' *what in tarnation does this have to do with the story you just told us?*

I'm gettin' there. I promise.

When I had lived 71.6 years, I marked that time in my life as significant.

This is why.

The stars had precessed one degree in the night sky in my lifetime.

I have been alive to witness this.

Put another way, we can see by observing the night sky that the stars rise in the east and move across the sky toward the west if we are watching them in our southern sky. But, ever so slightly, they are also moving "backward" from west to east.

IT TAKES 71.6 YEARS FOR THE STARS TO MOVE ONE DEGREE FROM WEST TO EAST, CAUSING THE PRECESSION OF THE EQUINOXES.

It's imperceptible in one lifetime, but over 1,000 years, you couldn't fail to see it.

Up to this point, there is a general consensus that the Earth spins, orbits the Sun, and is tilted on its axis. It does rock back and forth and orbits the entire galaxy that is part of the solar system of the Sun. These are the four distinct ways the Earth is moving.

THE POINT IS ... I HAVE DONE SOME TRAVELIN' IN MY DAY, RIDIN' ON THE EARTH, AWARE OF ALL ITS MOVEMENTS. THE VIEWS HAVE BEEN SPECTACULAR AND HAVE ENRICHED MY SOUL, MAKING ME FEEL CONNECTED WITH THE UNIVERSE.

I am sad to say that, for the most part, we have lost touch with the natural world, with the night sky, and with all the wonders of both.

I believe that moral, physical, mental, and spiritual health and well-being have been the price we have paid. The evidence of that is within us and all around us. What used to be common knowledge now seems profound. Nobody seems able to see the obvious anymore.

Of course, there have been times in my life when I fought the urge to say, "Somebody, stop this thang. I want off." But, I chose life and continued my awe-inspiring journey.

My day will come when the ride is over.

As the song says, "Some glad morning when this life is over, I'll fly away." Even then, it won't be the end of my travels, but the beginning of my eternal journey, free from the restraints of this life. I'm sure there will be wonders to behold, which now, I can't fathom.

And I'll get to see my daddy.

*If you're interested in reading the works of the authors I used as the primary sources of information, I can assure you that you'll enjoy yourself. Graham Hancock is a fountain of information. I greatly enjoyed *Fingerprints of the Gods.* I also invite you to read *The Lost Star of Myth and Time* by Walter Cruttenden, who pointed out the laws of precession within our solar system. Swami Sri Yukteswar was a late 19th- early 20th-century Indian guru who wrote *The Holy Science.* He points out the ancient belief of the precession of equinoxes and world ages which, as you can tell, I find endlessly fascinating. I hope you will, too.

Mules Love Turnips

Some folks will pay big bucks to see a pro football game.
Me? I'd just as soon watch a
couple of mules fightin' for a turnip.

ARE YOU FRUSTRATED, PILGRIM?

"A single act of kindness throws out roots in all directions,
and the roots spring up and make new trees."
~Amelia Earhart

I recently talked with a fellow traveler and veteran brother who felt overwhelming frustration.

In fact, he actually used that word.

After explaining what was troubling him, he asked me a question I am so often asked in one form or another.

"What can I do?"

As I am wont to do, I answered the question with a question.

"What do you think? I'd like to know what's on your mind as a possible course of action, so I can give you a more thoughtful response to your question."

His answer was, more or less, to restate the problem and the need he felt to "do something."

To begin with, no one person is going to change the world or make everyone live together in peace, love, harmony, agreement, and goodwill. If you choose to carry that weight on your shoulders, you will always feel frustrated.

But, I did answer his question.

I explained that all of us have a circle of influence; yes, some circles are larger than others, but we all have one.

YOU are within the circle. Start with YOU. Be the kind of person who would contribute to the solution. This will give you credibility and moral authority in influencing others in your circle—maybe just your family and friends.

That's something.

THAT MIGHT BE ALL YOU CAN DO, BUT IF MILLIONS OF LIKE-MINDED PEOPLE DO THE SAME, IT CREATES AN IRRESISTIBLE FORCE.

Picture a young private, in a great, global war, with millions of people opposing each other on many fronts. If our private feels the fate of the world depends on him, or even the outcome of the battle, he will think in terms of a circle of influence far outside his ability to sway.

So, what can our private do?

First, he can steel his mind with resolve. We know he has a field of fire—just a tiny little piece of real estate in the grand scheme of things. This means he can ensure any opposing forces that enter will have a bad day. It stands to reason if everyone does the same, there will be victory.

We can't make everyone in the world be nice to their dog, but we can be nice to ours.

We can't stop everyone in the world from mistreating horses, but we can treat ours well.

We can't feed all the hungry children in the world, but we can feed ours.

We can't make everyone in the world love one another, but we can love the folks in our circle.

You get the point. As always, the answers come from within you.

Frustration is a state of mind that makes you feel powerless, but in your neck of the woods, that is never true. Be content, and find joy in knowing you are doing all you can do in your circle.

Success comes when like-minded folks do what they can, where they are. Frustration comes when our focus is on that which is beyond our control. This man was peering past the edges of his circle, so he was feeling out of his element to the degree it was making him nuts.

Do you see yourself here from time to time?

Time to adjust fire then.

Sometimes There's No Other Way

Some things you say and do in life are like licking something good off a sharp knife. There's a right and wrong way.

LIGHTEN UP

"Should you ever find yourself the victim of other people's bitterness, smallness, or insecurities, remember, things could be worse. You could be them."
~ Unknown

There is nothing to be gained by being disagreeable with disagreeable people.

Learn to "let things slide," hold your tongue, smile, and move on. Say what you mean, and mean what you say, but know that some will disagree with you when you do.

They have as much a right to express themselves as you do. If they are rude, disrespectful, or unkind, that's all the more reason to just smile and move on.

Don't allow yourself to be drawn into a senseless debate that will end up being nothing more than a "peeing" contest without a winner.

Lighten up!

Pick Your Battles

Make some memories, and remember,
nobody ever won an argument.

ARE YOU WORRIED?

"Whatever is going to happen will happen
whether we worry or not."
~Ana Monnar

Are you worried?

Worry is projecting yourself into the future and assuming the worst.

Hopefulness is projecting yourself into the future and assuming the best.

Since we don't know what the future holds, why not assume the best? It's your choice.

Memories are Selective

Making memories is a good thang,
but winning an argument will never be one.

THELMA, SPUDS, AND BELLY RUBS

"All good animals have secret lives."
~Kate Bernheimer

Well, it's been a good day at Round Mountain.

NOW IT'S ROCKIN' CHAIR TIME, SIPPIN' TIME, AND THINKIN' TIME.

All the critters got their belly rubs and are feeling mellow and easy. Thelma and Spuds got into a might of a tiff at the RMCC meeting but settled their issue without me having to intervene. That's a good thang.

Floyd has been trying to spark up Thelma of late, and she has been teasing him, for sure.

They'll be taking some time off here soon. If you're married, I know you know what I mean.

Okay, y'all best be headin' back where ya came from. I'm fixin' to do some serious ponderin' 'bout some stuff I need to get sorted out.

You're Only as Good as Your Tools

A knife that won't cut isn't worth much.

Bo's a Good Kitty in a Storm

"In ancient times, cats were worshipped as gods;
they have not forgotten this."
~ Terry Pratchett

I spent some time with Bo, one of my Round Mountain kitties, this week.

He heads up the Kittie Brigade, which is charged with force recon missions in the event of hostilities at Round Mountain. Bo is a good kitty in a storm; make no mistake. He works closely with the Bird Brigade, commanded by Buzz Buzzard, whose all-seeing eyes will provide ample warning of pending action.

With that, I can't write anymore because Bo wants a belly rub, and I ain't got nothing else to say to ya.

Look Up

In life, only a few things are truly important.
Most thangs that are makin' your shorts ride up are
just belly button lint or hen poop on a pump handle.

ROUND MOUNTAIN BABIES

"Always be on the lookout for the presence of wonder."
~E.B. White

I just got back from Round Mountain and checking in with all my critters.

We called a special meeting of the RMCC to discuss some issues with the RMCCC (Round Mountain Critter Code of Conduct).

Thelma and Floyd were there with little Christine, and a lot of critters showed up with their new babies. Spuds and Ethel showed up with twelve little piggies, and things got a little out of hand there, with the babies overrunnin' everthang, but it was all good.

Babies make me smile and wear me out. Afterward, I settled back for some rockin' chair time, had a smoke, a snort, did some thinkin', and some readin'.

I took a long walk in the woods, and a whip-poor-will sang me to sleep last night. Good times that put me in the right mood.

Trust Yourself More

Trust your gut. If you think something doesn't
make a lick of sense, you're probably right.

DON'T GO BAT POOP CRAZY

"You yourself, as much as anybody in the entire universe,
deserve your love and affection."
~ Buddha

Listen up, you lovers. There's lots of negative emotions. Some, such as unforgiveness, loneliness, worry, and stress, are internalized, eat away at your insides, and rob you of hope and joy in life.

Others, such as hate, rage, jealousy, and greed, do the same but can also make you bat poop crazy and a danger to others. Git holt of yerselves, pilgrims.

Don't Wish for
War Stories

Be careful what you wish for. Folks who like war
stories most likely don't have their own to tell.

THELMA'S READY TO POP!

"I'll love you forever. I'll like you for always.
As long as I'm living, my baby you'll be."
~Robert Munsch

I'm headed to Round Mountain to see my critters. Thelma is due anytime—like no one noticed!

She's just like any pregnant mama and needs a good belly rub, so I'm on my way to make her more comfortable.

All right, I'm through with ya. Looking at you makes me want a snort or two.

Pay Up!

A rifle doesn't make you a Marine,
and a hat doesn't make you a cowboy.
There's dues to pay.

CRITTERS ARE PEACHY KEEN

"Really love your peaches.
Wanna shake your tree."
~ *"The Joker," The Steve Miller Band*

Critters are so thoughtful, especially deer.

I planted a small orchard at Round Mountain a few years ago to have fruit to share with them. Sure enough, when I went to check on it, they had saved me a peach.

It was delicious!

I guess they felt bad about eating all the plums.

Momma Didn't Raise No Crybabies

It's hard to take you seriously when you're acting like a spoiled brat whose mama wouldn't buy him some gummy bears.

THE BOND OF BLOOD

"I like to see people reunited. I like to see people run to each other. I like the kissing and the crying. I like the impatience, the stories that the mouth can't tell fast enough, the ears that aren't big enough, the eyes that can't take in all of the changes. I like the hugging, the bringing together, the end of missing someone."
—Jonathan Safran Foer

He had not yet arrived, but I knew he was coming.

Memories from long ago swirled through my mind; memories from a simpler time, mostly childhood memories, memories of people I had loved and who now were all gone.

All gone but one.

I had driven from Houston, Texas, to Georgetown, Ohio, to see him, trying to remember the last time I saw him. My memory failed me. It must have been about fifty years.

Then a pickup truck came into view as it rounded a curve. My gut told me it was him. Sure enough, the pickup slowed, turned into the driveway, and pulled off into the grass by the barn.

THE DRIVER'S DOOR OPENED, AND AN OLD MAN EMERGED.

The years had taken their toll, and I would have never recognized him after all this time, but I knew it was him. Time had gotten in a few good licks on me, too. He wouldn't recognize me either.

As he walked to the back of his truck, he turned his back to me and the others who had gathered for this special day. Then he dropped the tailgate of his truck and reached for something as I walked up behind him.

"You'd be my Uncle Donny," I said.

The old man turned around and looked at me. My heart seemed overwhelmed with what I can only describe as absolute and total love for this old man who now stood before me.

"I'm Charles, Charles' boy."

I extended my hand, smiling but fighting back tears.

He paused for a moment, looking at me as if trying to get his mind around what had just happened to him. Ignoring my hand, he stepped forward and embraced me in a big bear hug, which I returned. After a long embrace, we pulled back and looked at each other.

HAPPY TEARS FLOWED FROM BOTH OUR EYES.

We embraced again and then made our way over to all the others who had gathered for what I call the Kentucky Hamm Clan Reunion.

My grandfather, Charles Henry Hamm, had seven children, five boys and two girls. My daddy, also Charles, was the third of the seven. Donny was the baby of the family and now the only one still with us. He was the patriarch of the Kentucky Clan now.

When I first attended the reunion three years ago, I walked into a world of mostly strangers who I had never met and others I had not seen since I was a child. I was equally a stranger to them.

But a wonderful dynamic played out on that amazing day. I met these "strangers." They were first cousins I had never known and their children and grandchildren. They were the extended families of my aunts and uncles.

When I attended that reunion, I brought with me my own memories. These are the people dearest to me, including all my cookie bandits.

The connections we all shared through those seven children of Charles Henry created a bond of blood. Hugs, firm handshakes, tears, and much laughter were the order of the day. Lots of stories were told.

These folks made me feel so special. They all knew each other, of course. But I was the real stranger.

They wanted to know all about me and my memories of their mothers and fathers—my aunts and uncles. Charles Henry, my grandfather, had died when I was nine years old, but I had memories of him. They were hungry for stories about him as well.

What a day it turned out to be!

I have faithfully attended the reunion for three straight years now. It is not quite the same as the first time.

WE AREN'T STRANGERS NOW.
WE'RE FAMILY, BOUND BY BLOOD.

If you've lost touch with extended family, I wish such a day for each of you. You'll make some treasured memories and never regret stopping time to enjoy them.

Don't Lose Your Cool

The reasons you might have for being upset
are the very reasons you should remain calm.
Clear heads always prevail when stuff gets crazy.

HEAVEN IS A MOUNTAIN

"Among the clouds, we shared a cup of tea,
the mountain and me."
~Meeta Ahluwalia

It is the simple things that calm our spirits, help us put things in perspective, and bring us peace.

There is nothing, for me, quite like sitting on the front porch of the cabin in the evening as the Sun is setting, watching the hummingbirds, the critters that come to visit, and listening to the birds sing for me.

THESE ARE THE BEST OF TIMES.
HERE I AM IN AN ALTERNATE REALITY.
OH, YEAH, A SNORT OF JACK GOES WELL, TOO.

I'll be headed to Round Mountain soon to spend four days lost in the woods. God told me not long ago that it had crossed His mind to just send me up here when I die.

He looks out for me and has for a long time. I didn't always realize it, but He was always there.

I'm grateful.

If you ask me why there's no place I'd rather be than Round Mountain, I'll smile and remain silent.

I guess my heaven is Round Mountain. I hope after sharing bits of my story with you that you can see parts of your heaven there, too.

TEXAS GRIT TO
STICK IN YOUR CRAW

"Life Lessons"

THE HIGH COST OF ANGER

"Before you wrap up your day and go to bed, forget about those people who make you angry. Remember those who make you smile and go to bed with a smile." - Unknown

I recently wrote about the problem some people have with anger, defining it as a lack of self-control.

NOW, IF WE ARE BEING HONEST WITH OURSELVES, ANGER SHOWS WEAKNESS, NOT STRENGTH.

I also wrote about my wonderful Grandpa and the heart-lifting memories I have of him in the last chapter. I told the story of how he lived and how he died—shot and killed in an argument with another man.

Here's the article the *Carlisle Mercury* wrote about him on October 19, 1955. A dear contact I had barely known became engrossed in the story and couldn't help herself from finding this treasure.

It reads:

Nicholas County Man Slain in Argument

CARLISLE, Ky. (AP) A 66-year-old Nicholas County painter and farmer was slain near here Sunday in what authorities said was the climax to an argument over the disappearance of some tools.

Dead was Charles Henry Hamm, who lived in the county's Ellisville community. Deputy Sherriff Maurice Cameron said a murder charge was filed against Clinton Myers, 44, Nicholas County.

Cameron said the shooting occurred at Myers' home.

He gave this account, as related to by Myers and witnesses:

Hamm came to Myers' home and said he had located some of his missing tools in an outbuilding there. An argument ensued, and Myers obtained a single-shot .22 caliber rifle. He and Hamm scuffled over the weapon, and Hamm was shot in the abdomen.

Nicholas County Man Slain In Argument

CARLISLE, Ky. UP—A 66-year-old Nicholas County painter a n d farmer was slain near here Sunday in what authorities said was the climax to an argument over the disappearance of some tools.

Dead was Charles Henry Hamm, who lived in the county's Ellisville c o m m u n i t y. Deputy Sheriff Maurice Cameron said a murder charge was filed against Clinton Myers, 44, Nicholas County.

Cameron said the shooting occurred at Myers' home.

He gave this account, as related by Myers and witneses:

Hamm came to Myers' home and said he had located some of his missing tools in an outbuild i n g there. An argument ensued, and Myers obtained a single-shot .22 caliber rifle. He and Hamm scuffled over the weapon and Hamm was shot in the abdomen.

Article about Grandpa's death.
Carlisle Mercury, October 19, 1955.[1]

After Grandpa was shot, he managed to get into his truck and drive himself home. It was about ten miles to his house. He pulled into his yard, got out of his truck, and started making his way to the house. But he didn't make it. Grandpa collapsed in the yard. The family managed to get him to a doctor in Carlisle, but he died shortly thereafter.

---

1 "Nicholas County Man Slain in Argument." Carlisle Mercury. October 19, 1955.

I have often wondered what was going through his mind as he drove home. Many things, I'm sure. But he must have been reflecting on the series of decisions he'd made that day which had brought him to the awful place in which he found himself; decisions he made in anger.

Grandpa had begun his day in the peace and tranquility of a river-bank, fishing. Then he wound up driving home with a gunshot wound that would be fatal.

Why?

WHEN YOU BOIL IT ALL DOWN, CLEAR OUT ALL THE SELF-SERVING WEEDS, AND GET TO THE TRUTH, IT ALL HAPPENED BECAUSE GRANDPA GOT MAD.

I shared the article that appeared in the *Carlisle Mercury* because I feel Grandpa would want me to learn this lesson. He would want me to make it a part of his legacy.

It's not what happens to you in life. It's all about how you respond.

Learn Jesus and Josey

Sometimes, in life, it is wise to ask, "What would Jesus do?"
At other times, "What would Josey Wales do?"

Now, if you don't know who Jesus and Josey are,
we need to talk, pilgrims.

"GRANDPA, WERE YOU A HERO?"

*"Grandchildren are the dots that connect
the lines from generation to generation."*
~Lois Wyse

"Grandpa, were you a hero?" was a question one of my grandsons asked me not long ago. He was starting to hear things from the other kids and, perhaps, his parents. He knew I was a Marine veteran and was now old enough to understand a little about what that might have meant.

I smiled at the question, of course, and answered kindly, "No, I wasn't."

I then paused for a moment, reflecting, I suppose, then added, "But I knew some."

Without realizing it, he touched a nerve with me about the meaning of words.

There are words in all languages that distinguish some people from others. They are honorifics and superlatives that are intended to be reserved for only a few very exceptional people. But the words lose their meaning when applied to all, as is common today.

However, superlatives should be used thoughtfully and sparingly to protect the integrity of the word.

If everyone is "special," no one is special.

If everyone is "exceptional," no one is exceptional.

If everyone is "great," no one is great.

If everyone is a "hero," no one is a hero.

This brings me to the point of my answer to my grandson. I have strong feelings about what he brought up.

Because if everyone who wears, or has worn, the uniform of our military services is a "hero," what does the word even mean? It is reduced to mean nothing more than: "A person who served in the armed forces."

If that is the case, then how will we designate those few who truly rose to a level of extraordinary courage above and beyond the call of duty?

This is why I'll stick with the word "hero" when I think of such people.

No, I'm not one, but I knew some.

Me?

I'm a Marine veteran who did his duty. That's it.

You old vets understand.

If you are one, you get it.

If you aren't, trust me on this.

Tighty-Whitey Wisdom

Never let the skivvies you wore
today smell up your tomorrow.

CORPORAL JOHN ROBERT DAYTON, REST IN PEACE

"Unable are the loved to die, for love is immortality."
~Emily Dickinson

*This story contains references to suicide. If you are in crisis, call the National Suicide Prevention Lifeline at 800-273-8255.

I stood with a sense of deep reverence for several moments. I was finally here and had found what I was looking for. I had driven from Houston to El Paso, Texas, for only one reason. It was for this moment in time. I wanted to find the grave of Army Corporal John Robert Dayton to pay my respects.

SHOULD TEARS COME TO MY EYES, I WOULD MAKE NOT THE SLIGHTEST ATTEMPT TO HOLD THEM BACK.

Now, you might be wondering why an old Marine Sergeant would be snapping to attention and giving an old Army Corporal a salute, why he would maybe shed a tear.

There is a reason. There is a story here.

Corporal Dayton is buried at the military cemetery at Fort Bliss. He had joined the Army in 1897 and had served in the 12th US Infantry in Cuba during the Spanish American War. He died on 23 October 1903, at Fort Bliss—just twenty-four years old.

BUT I'M GETTING AHEAD OF MYSELF. THIS IS WHERE THE STORY ENDS. LET'S GO BACK TO THE BEGINNING.

Corporal Dayton was born and raised on a farm in Robertson County, Kentucky. His father, John Robert Dayton, Sr., fought in the Union Army during the Civil war. On 27 July 1878, as I told you, he was murdered by a band of regulators. His wife, Caroline, was two months pregnant with their sixth child at the time of his death. She gave birth to a baby boy on 14 February 1879 and named him after his father. John Robert, Sr., and Caroline are my great-great-grandpa and grandma, so, you see, Corporal Dayton was my great uncle.

We are bonded by blood. We're family.

I had several reasons to make the pilgrimage to his gravesite. Perhaps, the most important to me was my certainty that not one family member, people who loved or would have loved him, had ever visited his grave. I would be the first one.

I saluted him smartly. I then imagined he was there with me in spirit and introduced myself, making the family connection for him. I ran the family tree from him back to me and spoke of being a fellow veteran, how I had come close to dying as he had—but didn't.

I had been there with him for about forty-five minutes and had been okay up to that point. But when I asked him about his death, a sadness settled into my soul.

Yes, I teared up. "Why, Uncle John? Why? Help me understand."

Silence.

I then "went Marine sergeant" on him. Heck, I outranked him, and I wanted to know.

"CORPORAL DAYTON, I ASKED YOU A BLANK, BLANK QUESTION, AND I WANT A BLEEPIN' ANSWER. NO RESPONSE, BUT I HAD A SENSE MY THEATRICS MADE HIM CHUCKLE. I HAD TO SMILE.

His death had been the ultimate tragedy. He'd been so young and had never married or fathered children. I knew the "what" but not the "why."

My great uncle had committed suicide and taken his reasons to his grave.

His legacy became broken-hearted people who loved and would have loved him. It reached across generations to his great-nephew, standing at his grave, tearing up a little—wondering why.

Git Yer Hand Off That

If something doesn't need messin' with, don't mess with it.

LISTEN UP, BOOGER BOYS AND GIRLS

"Boy, the solid things you can hold in your hands are never all you've got. They're the least of what belongs to you. The qualities inside you, those are what you've really got to defend yourself with."
~Traci L. Slatton

It was a perfect moment in time.

I sat in my rocking chair, surveying my domain. My whole body, inside and out, felt like one big smile.

SCATTERED BEFORE ME, ALL MY COOKIE BANDITS HAD GONE FERAL, RUNNING WILD IN THE WOODS, UNSUPERVISED, LOOKING FOR BIGFOOT TRACKS.

They were having a great time.

Life was good.

Suddenly, I could tell something had gone horribly wrong. My youngest grandson, Lucas, then about four years old, came running to me, jumped into my lap, and put his arms around me. He sobbed uncontrollably.

I asked him what was wrong.

He answered through his sobs, "Sophie called me a booger boy."

I waited until he calmed down, then said, "Well, let me ask you a question. Are you a booger boy?"

He answered emphatically, "NO, Grandpa. I'm NOT a booger boy."

I said, "I agree with you. I don't think you are either. So if you know you aren't one, and Grandpa agrees with you, then what she said isn't true, is it?"

We talked on. Me doing the best I could with a four-year-old boy, trying to make him understand that he should not let what other people say define him when what they say isn't true. "Ignore such things," I insisted, smiling into his tear-stained face.

Lucas felt insulted and offended, but I have often noted through the years how childish adults become under similar circumstances.

They get pouty, angry, hostile, resentful, and wounded in spirit.

NOW, LET ME ASK YOU:
WHY WOULD YOU ALLOW THE UNKIND WORDS OF ANOTHER TO HAVE SUCH POWER OVER YOU?

In this chapter's title, I called y'all booger boys and girls. If you happen to be one, perhaps you should take note. If you're not one, why would you care?

Check Again

If right or wrong is just what you think,
nothing is right or wrong.

WHY HATE WILL FAIL YOU

"Hate is like burning down your own
house to get rid of a rat."
~Henry Emerson Fosdick

It's one thing to disagree with someone, oppose them, or even resist them. It is an altogether different thing to hate them. Hate may prevail for a time but is doomed to fail. It consumes those it captivates as a poison to their soul. Wise, rational behavior, or thought, will not be found in its victims. Loving one another is a better way, even if you disagree.

Perspective

Often it's how you look at things that's the issue.
Everybody thought Goliath was too big to hit.
David thought he was too big to miss.

SPENDING QUALITY
TIME WITH YOURSELF

"Nothing can bring you peace but yourself."
~Ralph Waldo Emerson

As I told you, back in September, I attended a reunion of a family clan from Ohio and Kentucky. It was held in Georgetown, Ohio.

I spent four full days, and part of another, on the road and in motel rooms. When I returned, my guys on the job site asked me about it and seemed pleased that I had a good time.

**THEN ONE ASKED ME A QUESTION THAT
MADE THEM ALL, ME INCLUDED, LAUGH.
"MR. C., DID YOU LISTEN TO THE RADIO?"**

My guys give me a hard time because I never turn on the radio. I hadn't really thought about it, but I had driven all that way, about 2,400 miles, and had not once turned it on.

I answered the question with a smile, "No, come to think of it. I didn't."

They were amazed but not surprised. "Mr. C., you just ain't right. What did you do?"

I replied, "I was thinking."

"What were you thinking about for all that time?"

"Women," I answered and was met with howls of laughter.

I continued, "Actually, I spent some time wondering if our Sun, along with our solar system, is in a binary orbit with another star and how its gravity might influence planetary orbits, the Earth's ocean tides, and the lithosphere during periapsis."

I found myself staring into the faces of a bunch of dead-eyed mouth breathers, so it was time to get to work.

I am not a reclusive loner. I love good company and good conversation.

However, I have always cherished time alone and make time for solitude. I have never been a man who needs to be entertained. Most of what you hear on the radio and see on TV, especially the moronic commercials, is nothing but nonsense anyway. We fill our lives with meaningless distractions and avoid coming to grips with ourselves.

The sages, through the ages, have intoned: "Know thyself," or some equivalent.

I agree.

A well-lived and fulfilling life begins with knowing exactly who we are. We *need* time for self-reflection. We *need* to work on ourselves. We *need* time to think and ponder on what's really important to us.

Your reveries will take you many places and will tell you a great deal about who you really are and what you need to work on to become a better person. Your thoughts will paint a very clear picture of you if you take time to think about them.

It is important that you like what you see.

IF YOU DON'T LIKE THE PICTURE, IDENTIFY WHY THEN GET BACK TO WORK ON IT. MAKE IT A MASTERPIECE.

We hear of spending quality time with others. It is just as important to spend quality time with ourselves.

Outsmart 'Em

If you must fight the tiger,
don't make it a contest of fangs and claws.

FLAWED MAN

"I myself am made entirely of flaws,
stitched together with good intentions."
~Augusten Burroughs

I am a flawed man, but I work on myself and try to improve.

Over the years, I have made up little sayings in this regard that have served me well. I sometimes share them with people who will listen. One is:

"KNOWLEDGE IS KNOWING YOU CAN GO WHEN THE LIGHT TURNS GREEN. WISDOM IS MAKING SURE EVERYONE HAS STOPPED BEFORE YOU DO."

Yesterday morning about 0530, that saying served me well.

I was sitting at a red light, waiting to make a left turn. When the light turned green, I paused for a second and glanced to my left. A car, going at least seventy miles per hour, I guessed, on a city street with a speed limit of thirty-five, was running the red light. It was gone in a flash. Had I not paused and looked but accelerated into the intersection, I would surely have been T-boned.

I've seen the sweet chariot swing in low in my day, but it wasn't coming for me. That instance, however, gave me pause yesterday morning.

Although the saying mentioned above illustrates the difference between knowledge and wisdom, it is true.

Driving is likely the most dangerous thing you do. BE SAFE, DANG IT!!

You Don't Know Everything

It's foolish to dismiss something as false
simply because you don't know it to be true.

MODERATION

"Everything in moderation, including moderation."
~ Oscar Wilde

Let me encourage you, if you drink, to do so moderately and responsibly.

Here is how to tell if you have reached your limits: if you pour yourself another shot, spill a little on the table, and lick it up—you've had enough.

Think Again

Keep an eye on the "know-it-all."
Maybe it's just me, but some of the dumbest
people I know are folks who "know everything."

BELLY RUBS AND FREEDOM

"America will never be destroyed from the outside.
If we falter and lose our freedoms,
it will be because we destroyed ourselves."
~Abraham Lincoln

I find it very strange that people who live under the boot of tyranny and dependence dream of living free, while those who live free and independent dream of tyranny and dependence.

This is Rex, another of my Round Mountain dogs. Rex, like me, lives free and will die free. He asks for nothing else. He has no desire to be caged or chained.

Oh, and he likes belly rubs, too, but not at the expense of his freedom.

P.S. I spoke to Rex about his pedigree, and he swears he's a dog. Case closed.

More Listenin', Less Talkin'

Don't talk loud, don't talk fast,
and don't talk often.

Prepare for the Future

"An hour of thinking can save a decade of struggle."
~Johnny Ozan

One is wise who finds peace and contentment in the present. However, you still need to prepare for the future.

Winter will come, and when it does, you don't want to be cutting wood; you want to enjoy the fire.

Now, my critters are coming down the mountain to get belly rubs, and I got stuff to do. So, ponder on it, pilgrims. It's important.

Don't Pop Off

When everybody else is angry and getting crazy,
that's all the more reason for you to stay calm.

Dollars and Sense

"Money grows on the tree of persistence."
~ Japanese proverb

Few things in life cause more stress than financial matters.

Thank goodness there are two truths to follow to ease this particular pain.

Remember this:

1. There is no such thing as a free lunch, and you must pay your bills.

2. A quick search of the internet tells us that financial matters are the second leading cause of divorce, according to statistical studies. So get your finances right to preserve your relationship.

I have written on this subject before, emphasizing the importance of never spending or committing all your money until you are as dry as a dog's favorite, well-gnawed bone.

You must save money for the unexpected.

The average American knows little about the basic principles of managing their money. The problem is only made worse by our "culture of spending," and the temptation so many have to impress.

Let me recommend this book to you: "The Millionaire Next Door" by Thomas J. Stanley and William D. Danko. It can be life-changing if you let it.

Do let it.

Did You Catch That?

If brains were money, and you could go around the
world for a dime, some folks couldn't get out of sight.

STRONG ENOUGH TO BE HUMBLE

"Humility is nothing but truth,
and pride is nothing but lying."
~Saint Vincent de Paul

I don't know what the circumstances were or what actually happened. In fact, it had nothing to do with me and was none of my business.

But what I overheard gave me a sense of sadness. A young boy, maybe, twelve years old, approached a man I took to be his father. His dad was a big, tough-looking guy.

They both seemed upset. Then the boy spoke.

"Dad, I'm sorry."

The father, leaning down toward the boy, scolded, "Don't *ever* say you're sorry, and don't *ever* say you're wrong. It shows weakness."

What a thing for a father to say to a little boy.

If one makes a mistake, whether in word or deed, that adversely affects others, it is proper to acknowledge it. A person who will not is morally and mentally weak. They are insecure, troubled souls. False, stubborn pride and self-righteousness will enslave them.

We need to bring back the concept of being a gentleman. We are losing it. There is no contradiction in being strong, tough, and immovable in the breach on the day of adversity while also being a humble, gentle soul who is strong enough to be real in polite society.

HUMILITY SHOULD SERVE TO BALANCE THE SHARPER EDGES OF NATURAL MASCULINITY AND MAKE US "GENTLE MEN."

This is what real men should teach their sons. I'm thinking the ladies will agree.

Some Folks Think They Know

When someone speaks in a confusing manner, two things should be immediately obvious: It is nothing profound, and the speaker doesn't know what they're talking about.

Living in Fear

"Too many of us are not living our dreams
because we are living our fears."
~ Les Brown

Fear is comparable to what we might think of as a possession.

It is a self-destructive, all-consuming "spirit" that will paralyze your body and soul.

It is a foreboding, fed by thoughts that something terrible might happen to you.

It could be any number of things.

WORRY, FEAR, AND TERROR ARE RELATED. WORRY CAN LEAD TO FEAR, AND FEAR CAN MAKE YOU TERRIFIED. THE LATTER IS FEAR ON STEROIDS.

First, you must identify the root cause that is making you fearful. You must ask yourself, "Why am I afraid?"

You must understand that life is not without risks.

Failure to face this will make life not worth living. We become the living dead.

I recently wrote that I will not live in fear of getting sick. (I made no reference to any particular illness, but everyone assumed I meant a certain one.) Nor will I live in fear of having an accident or heart attack —which my genes make likely. I'm not afraid that I might get cancer or some other awful disease. I'm not afraid I might have high blood pressure and have a stroke. I'm not afraid of being a victim of crime or being murdered. I'm not afraid of the critters rustling about behind me right now.

I could go on.

I choose to be content, play out the hand I was dealt, and live and love life until the ultimate fate of us all comes calling for me.

I might add, I'm not afraid to die.

I like living this way. Ponder on it, Pilgrims.

A Fool and a Wise Man

A fool trusts in his strength and doesn't know his weaknesses.
The wise know their strength, never fail to take their
shortcomings into account, and make provision for them.

KEEP YOUR HEAD

"It is a living death if one is obsessed by pride,
ego, and anger."
~Sathya Sai Baba

So ya say ya have a bad temper?

Is that supposed to be an excuse for bein' ill-mannered, sayin' dumb stuff, and actin' like a fool when somethin' doesn't go your way, or someone says somethin' you don't like?

I don't buy it.

Your temper ain't the problem. You lack self-control. You're weak between the ears. When a cool head is most important, you go stupid. I ain't got much time for ya. Ya can't be counted on in a storm.

Note: I actually said this to a hot-headed man several years back. I ran into him not long ago, and he told me what I said to him had changed his life. He thanked me. Made me feel good.

Grow a Pair

Take note of the timid and fearful.
They might agree with you, in principle,
but will not have your back in the day of adversity.

THE TROUBLE WITH THE TRUTH

"In the long run, the most unpleasant truth is a
safer companion than a pleasant falsehood."
~ Theodore Roosevelt

Ever wonder why it seems folks hate the truth? Well, the trouble with the truth is it's neutral; it has no agenda. It stands flat-footed, looks us squarely in the eyes, and will never blink.

It is what it is.

It can't be anything else and won't be anything else.

It is incapable of compromise, always standing immovable.

It is never wrong.

It is never a lie.

It is absolute, and absolutes make us uncomfortable.

Truth doesn't care what you think. It doesn't care what I think. It never bends or yields. It doesn't agree with you. It demands you agree with it. It doesn't come searching for you. It demands you search for it. It doesn't stand with you. You must stand with it.

Truth stands in judgment to the folly of us all but blesses those whose quest in life is to find it and embrace it.

Are You Overthinking This?

If you don't know something,
it doesn't mean there isn't something to know.

WHO IS THE WORST
BOSS IN THE WORLD?

"I haven't really had too many bad bosses. Any bad boss I
had probably was because I was a bad employee."
~Jason Sudeikis

I usually make a point to read most things posted on the subject of
leadership.

Most often, it is some high-minded point about what good leaders
do or don't do. I have not read any that seem to be describing me, my
approach to doing business, or my attitude toward my employees.

THEREFORE, I HAVE CONCLUDED
I AM A TERRIBLE LEADER.

I believe that my first responsibility is to my clients. When they give
me work, they become my boss, and my job is to provide excellent
service to them and for them, so they can feel like they got their money's
worth when they get the invoice.

My first responsibility is not to the people who work for me. They
must feel responsible to me, just as I do to my bosses/clients.

I do not hire people because I want to "help them." I hire people
because I want them to help me. I have work to get done and can't do it
all myself. When I hire someone, I tell them what they will be doing,
and we agree to what I will pay them. I did not start the business to
create jobs. Jobs are the natural outgrowth of a successful business.

I think my greatest failure is putting "profits before people." That is a bad thing.

That means you are making money, and if you are, you should be "giving back." I don't have the slightest idea what that is supposed to mean, but we are supposed to put people before profits.

While clients are always first in my mind, and I want them to be totally happy with the service I provide, I still want to make a buck.

If I don't make a profit, I cannot pay my employees, and then there is no job. If I don't make a profit, I can't afford to expand the business, buy more equipment, and create additional jobs.

IF I DON'T MAKE A PROFIT, I WON'T HAVE ANY MONEY IN MY JEANS TO BUY A NEW HAT EVERY YEAR OR MAINTAIN MY LAVISH, JET-SETTING LIFESTYLE.

My employees have the same responsibility to me as I have to my clients. The standard is excellence in what we do.

I see very little, if anything, that discusses the responsibility of the employee to his company. I get the impression that employers are to be some benevolent father-figure type to a bunch of spoiled children who think they should still get their allowance, even if they didn't make their bed.

I don't play that.

Let me note here that among other names, my guys do call me Mr. C., Uncle Charlie, and Pops. But Pops is a "tough love" kind of man.

I expect my people, in exchange for what I pay them, to do an excellent job.

I expect them to give me a good day of work.

I expect them to do what I tell them.

I expect them to be engaged in what we are doing, even to the point of disagreeing with me if they think I am wrong or there might be a better way.

And I don't mind good men making mistakes. We all do. It is my responsibility to catch mistakes and coach a man up so he'll do better next time.

But if someone wants to get a day of pay out of me, and is lazy, indifferent, irresponsible, doesn't care about the quality of his work, wants to text, or talk on the phone all day, is insubordinate, brings a lot of drama and confusion along with him, and generally violates the trust I put in him when I hired him, I'll fire his butt quicker than I can kiss a duck, go home, have some supper, hit the rack and sleep like a baby.

I told you, I'm a bad man.

Knowledge
is a Treasure

Pursue, and learn to appreciate the value of insight,
discernment, understanding, knowledge, and wisdom.
Herein will be found great treasure.

CURE-ALL FOR
FIRST-DAY JITTERS

"It takes only two years to learn to talk
but a lifetime to learn to keep your mouth shut."
~Anonymous

Look here, boys and girls, on your first day on the job, it's best to keep your mouth shut and look and listen.

If you see somebody who looks like he knows what he's doing, hang with him.

You might learn something.

Don't Ask a Donkey for Advice

Wisdom is unlikely to be found among those with no knowledge of history.

Priceless Lessons of Life

"You may all go to hell, and I will go to Texas."
~Davy Crockett

Priceless lessons of life are to be learned from forests, fields, and the wonders of the critters who call it home.

BLESSED IS ONE WHO FEELS A SENSE OF BELONGING HERE.

I'm the keeper of the legends and lore of Round Mountain, as you might have guessed.

The story I am about to tell you has been verified by the oral traditions handed down by the Round Mountain critters. Yep, it's true! Davy Crockett spent a month or so at Round Mountain when he first came to Texas.

While here, Davy killed a 'coon from a large white oak that's still here today, from which he made the hat that he wore at the Alamo.

That 'coon, Roscoe, selflessly gave his life so Davy would look his best when he got to The Alamo. He was the great-grandfather, many times removed, of Rocko, who frequently hangs from his favorite tree and does acrobatics to impress the rest of us.

104

As you might guess, Rocko is exceedingly proud of his heritage and is a true Texas Blue Blood at Round Mountain. Rocko and I are the only ones here that can claim direct ancestry to the Alamo. He now figures prominently in the defense of Round Mountain, but his mission is top secret.

Well now, I'm storied out, and this stuff really ain't none of your bidness. I just rambled on a bit as I'm wont to do now and then. So keep this between you and me. That's an order.

Think on It

Don't do something just because people say you can't.

HANK ASKS FOR NOTHING

"The price of greatness is responsibility."
~Winston Churchill

Ol' Hank, one of my Round Mountain rescue dogs, insists on taking full responsibility for himself.

He asks for nothing and expects nothing.

He makes his own way.

It's called freedom.

Now, I'm not saying Hank doesn't like a good belly rub, but it is always on his terms. I like Hank. Be like Hank.

Be Smarter Than
the Acorn

The way I see it, there ain't but two ways to git to the top of a big white oak tree. Ya ain't gotta be real bright to figure it out. You can climb it or sit on an acorn and wait.

ROOT HOGS OR DIE

"There are only two lasting bequests we can hope to give
our children. One of these is roots ... the other, wings."
~Henry Ward Beecher

I remember my daddy explaining how wild, domestic hogs got to be such a problem in many areas of Texas.

It seems that, many years ago, poor farmers would turn their hogs loose to have them fend for themselves. Hence, came the expression, "Root hog, or die."

Obviously, they did quite well as some never returned.

All the wild hogs at Round Mountain share the same fate.

Each will be summarily weaned by their mama with the same charge. They will have no choice but to fend for themselves and make their own way if they are to survive.

Our children should also reach a point in life where they understand they must leave the nest and take responsibility for themselves.

Failing to do this has caused many problems for recent, younger generations. Young folks don't seem to want to leave the protective care of their parents, and their parents are reluctant to let them go. This causes problems for both. It seems harsh, but it is nature's way.

Children must also be weaned.

THAT THE HILL YOU WANT TO DIE ON?

"Aka Wisdom"

WHO ARE YOU LISTENING TO?

"If I got rid of my demons, I'd lose my angels."
~ Tennessee Williams

I have two companions who have been with me for as long as I can remember.

I don't recall a time in my life, for even a moment, when they weren't there. In fact, I sometimes wonder if they didn't join me at birth, as if assigned to me by higher, competing, spiritual powers.

I have grown and changed over the years and have ultimately become an old man, now on the downside of seventy-five years. Yet, these passengers have stayed the same and been consistent to a fault.

One is a little demon that sits on my left shoulder.

The other is a little angel that sits on my right shoulder.

Each seems sworn to influence my life, and with each decision I must make, they offer diametrically opposing counsel. Of course, the decision is mine to make, but they compete for influence.

As a younger man, I listened more to the one on the left. His way was always easy, and it appealed more to my lesser man.

In time I realized he'd never had my best interest at heart and had advocated the way of a self-destructive fool. At about the same time, I started realizing the little angel on my right was wise, looked out for what was best for me, and taught me the way of wisdom and life without regret.

Now when faced with decisions, I have learned to listen to my angel.

This is not literally true, of course … or is it?

I have come to think this way about the competing influences that seem to be everywhere. There are powerful, contradictory forces at play in our world, struggling for control over our minds, but you choose who you listen to. It's all on you. Wisdom is the way of the good life. Choose wisely.

Slow Down

One day doesn't make a life one way or the other.
Take them one at a time and press on.

GRANDPA'S ASSIGNMENT

"Grandfathers are just antique little boys."
~ Unknown

As a grandpa, I'm always looking for opportunities to speak into the lives of my cookie bandits.

My interest is not so much what they do when they are grown. I try to focus on what kind of people they will become as adults.

They are well familiar with all of "Grandpa's sayings," of course, and have been for some time. But as they have gotten older, I can relate to them on a different level. Now, I want to encourage them to be wise. We talk a lot about it.

I RECENTLY TOLD MY GRANDSON, KOLTON, THAT HAPPINESS, INNER PEACE, CONTENTMENT, SELF-DISCIPLINE, KNOWLEDGE, UNDERSTANDING, AND LOVE FOR OUR FELLOW MAN ARE THE TREASURES OF THE WISE.

I urged him to always seek the company of those who find this treasure. But, I also encouraged him to be attentive to the ways of fools and never underestimate what you can learn from them. Observe their mannerisms, the consequences of their decisions, and be discerning. Learn from them, but never seek their counsel.

He then said to me, "Grandpa, you are a wise man." I smiled, and thanked him for the compliment, then continued.

"I recommend you study proverbs." He asked, "You mean the Book of Proverbs in the *Bible?*" I told him this would be a great place to start, but people the world over have their own proverbs. Proverbs are just brief statements of common sense; they are a great source of wisdom wherever you find them.

I then gave him an assignment and told him to read exactly what he had questioned me about—the Book of Proverbs in the *Bible*. I said, "After you read it, come back and tell me the two types of people who are repeatedly juxtaposed, and be prepared to discuss them with me."

I'M NOW GIVING EACH OF YOU THE SAME ASSIGNMENT.

Ponder on it, pilgrims.
I'll be waiting to hear from you.

One and Done

Never stress when life or work seems overwhelming.
Pick one thing that needs to be done, and get after it.

Has Wisdom Gone
by the Wayside?

"A symptom of wisdom is curiosity.
The evidence is calmness and perseverance.
The causes are experimentation and understanding."
~Maxime Lagacé

Today we often hear people described as smart, brilliant, experts, authorities, and such. Each term has a way of setting such people up on a level above the rest of us and implies that we should defer to them.

But, I have a question for you. "When was the last time you heard someone referred to as wise?"

As I've mentioned, we seem to have lost the concept of wisdom. It is not a consideration as we go about our daily lives and interface with others.

Being smart does not necessarily mean you are wise. I see highly intelligent people all about who live as absolute fools. Their deeds, words, thoughts, and hearts are given over to foolishness.

Wisdom demands we take knowledge and experience to its highest level, which will connect us to the spiritual realm that makes us truly human. Without wisdom, mankind can easily be reduced to self-destructive, self-serving, brutish barbarians.

That's one to ponder on. What will you do with it? What would a wise person do?

Keep Your Eye on Your Bobber

There's a time to work and a time to play.
Best not to mix the two.

WHY CROWS HATE OWLS

*"You reclaim your power by loving
what you were once taught to hate."
~Bryant H. McGill*

Most of the crows were still perched in the trees on the southern end of Round Mountain, where they had roosted the night before.

Dawn was breaking; the Sun would soon rise, and they were starting to stir. Only a few scouts had taken flight to get a jump on the day's activities, doing what crows do.

**MOST DAYS WERE ROUTINE, BUT A DRAMA
WOULD SOON UNFOLD THAT CROWS LIVE FOR,
A DRAMA THAT WOULD GIVE THEIR LIVES
MEANING FAR ABOVE MERE SURVIVAL.**

Cheyenne, a young crow, born only last spring, sat close to his mother, Cha Cha. Cheyenne was grown and independent of her but still stayed close. He was still young enough not to take the daily activities for granted. Every day was an adventure for him. It was nice to be with mom.

Oliver, a wise, old owl, sat on top of a fence post, quietly looking around at the lovely meadow filled with fall wildflowers. As he studied the eastern sky, he knew it was about time for him to be off to his den tree, where he would spend the day sleeping.

Oliver had a good life at Round Mountain. He kept to himself mostly and minded his own business. The other critters left him alone, and he didn't bother them. All the critters considered him wise and would turn to him for counsel from time to time. Sometimes he would advise them, but often he would not.

This only made Oliver seem the wiser to the critters of Round Mountain. Thelma, the undisputed matriarch and enforcer of the Round Mountain Critter Code of Conduct and chair of the Round Mountain Critter Council (RMCC), was second only to Mr. Charles (me).

When I was gone, Thelma could occasionally be seen meeting with Oliver. There appeared to be mutual respect between them.

But the peace Oliver enjoyed as he sat there was about to be shattered, and he knew it the moment he saw Comet, the leader of the crow clan. Oliver knew he had waited too long to retire to his den that morning. Comet had seen him and had sounded the crow's alarm.

CHAOS WOULD ENSUE, AND OLIVER JUST SHOOK HIS HEAD AS HE PREPARED FOR WHAT WAS COMING.

The air suddenly exploded in a blaring, ear-splitting din of "caws" as the ominous storm of crows, led by Comet, flew out of the woods. These caws were not normal but filled with hatred and rage. Little Cheyenne stayed close to his mother, confused by the mindless, raucous sounds and the frenzied attack by his family.

The crows dove down at Oliver repeatedly until they were all exhausted. Though having no idea what this was all about, Cheyenne joined in and made his own "dive-bombing" runs at the owl.

Soon enough, the crows retreated into the woods, and the owl made his way to his den. Cheyenne sat on a limb beside Cha Cha, gasping for breath. He was confused by what had happened and turned to his mother.

"Momma, why did we get so upset at the owl sitting on the fence post?"

"We're crows. We hate owls," replied Cha Cha.

"But why?" Cheyenne asked.

Cha Cha seemed a touch annoyed but responded, "I don't know. We just do. Crows hate owls, that's all. Maybe you should ask Comet, your grandfather."

Cheyenne purposed to do just that. He wanted to know. After the crows had settled down and recovered their strength, he flew over to the branch where Comet sat, still feeling the anger engendered by what had just transpired.

Cheyenne asked, "Grandpa Comet, why do we hate owls?"

Comet was nonplussed by the question and spoke with a harsh tone to his grandson. "You're a crow, and you ask me a stupid question like that?"

Cheyenne pressed on, to the annoyance of Comet, who quickly lost his patience with his grandson.

"I don't know, dang it, we just do. We're crows. If you're a crow, you hate owls. That's simply the way it is. Now, enough of your witless questions."

Cheyenne flew back to another branch, this time away from his mother. He wanted to think. He wanted an answer to his question, and "We just do" was not an answer. Rather, it was a statement of fact.

As he perched and thought, he realized that he had no reason to hate the owls. He was just *supposed* to hate them because everybody else did. *But why?*

There must be a reason. He determined to find the answer once and for all. Somebody ought to know.

Cheyenne went to his aunts and uncles and inquired of them. The response was the same among all of them. "I don't know. We're crows, and we hate owls. That's just the way it is."

The young crow realized that no one in his family would be a source for solving the mystery.

WEEKS PASSED AS CHEYENNE PONDERED HOW HE MIGHT FIND THE ANSWER TO THE MYSTERY. HE DIDN'T KNOW WHERE TO TURN.

Then one day, the crows caught Oliver out in the open again. They went wild with hate and anger. But, as they all dove at him repeatedly, Cheyenne held back.

He flew in circles as the others attacked, only watching, never participating. He simply didn't feel he had any reason to hate Oliver. In fact, if hatred made crows act so irrationally, he wanted no part of it.

He didn't want to hate anybody.

Several months later, Cheyenne was out alone.

He took note of a large white oak and settled on a limb to rest a spell. Then he noticed a den nearby in the trunk of the tree. His eyes caught movement. Momentarily Oliver, the owl, stuck his head out just far enough to look around. Their eyes met.

Cheyenne started to fly away, but something that could only be called a "eureka moment" stopped him cold. He thought, *maybe if I'm nice to him, I can ask him why crows hate owls. It couldn't hurt.*

Oliver was calm and unperturbed as he looked at Cheyenne closely.

He spoke matter of factly, "You're the young crow that didn't dive down on me when the rest of your family did."

Cheyenne nodded as Oliver grew silent, closely watching the young crow. Oliver's quiet observations of him made Cheyenne blurt out his question.

"Mr. Oliver, do you know why crows hate owls?"

Oliver decided to answer the question with a question.

"Why don't you ask your family?"

Cheyenne said with a tinge of frustration in his voice, "I have asked them all, and no one seems to have the slightest idea. I'm hoping maybe you know since we crows are so mean to you."

Oliver smiled and asked the young crow to come closer.

"Yes, the story has been handed down to me through countless generations. Unfortunately, the same is not true with you crows. If you agree to listen carefully, without interruption, I'll answer your question."

"I agree."

Oliver began to speak of a time many, many years ago when owls and crows liked each other. It was a time the Egyptians called sep tepi, which means "the first time." The Greeks called it the Golden Age, and it occurred about 12,000 years prior. This was in a time before a great flood, when animals, large beyond belief—mammoths, huge bear and beaver, and gigantic saber tooth cats, to name just a few—roamed about at Round Mountain.

Cheyenne listened carefully.

Oliver told how the leader of the crows, Conan, and the leader of the owls, Ollie, had been great friends at this time.

Then one day, Conan came to Ollie to compliment him on his well-known wisdom. He asked him to give advice on how he and his crow family could become wise.

"Speak less, and listen more," came Ollie's reply.

CONAN THOUGHT ABOUT THIS FOR A MOMENT, AND HIS TEMPER FLARED. HE CONSIDERED THIS TO BE AN INSULT, AND HATRED BOILED OVER IN HIS HEART.

He flew away without another word, rejoined his crow flock, and told them of the slanderous offense. Conan relayed that Ollie had said crows are loud-mouthed, obnoxious birds who should learn to shut up and listen.

He called for avenging this shame. The crows all flew to Ollie's den, caught him out on a limb, and dove on him. From then on, each generation taught the next generation to hate owls. After a while, nobody remembered why.

Cheyenne finally spoke. "You mean that crows hate you because of something that happened twelve thousand years ago?

"So it would seem," Oliver answered.

Cheyenne flew back to his flock and told the story he had heard from Oliver. He said emphatically that it was time to let this go. After a heated debate, the crows realized that Cheyenne was right. They felt foolish.

On that day, the crows of Round Mountain met with Oliver and the rest of the owls. Peace was made after centuries, much to the approval of all the Round Mountain critters.

The crows then learned of a nursery rhyme song that had been forbidden for them to even inquire about, for it spoke of the owl they had been taught to hate. Now, they laughed at themselves as they sang it to Oliver, who had taught it to them, and the owls, who all nodded and clucked with great joy.

"A wise old owl lived in an oak. The more he saw, the less he spoke. The less he spoke, the more he heard. Why can't we all be like that wise old bird?"

Because of his courage in seeking out the answer that changed the legacy of the crows and owls, when Cheyenne was old enough, he became the leader of the crows. For years, he has been revered by all the critters of Round Mountain for his wisdom.

Including one wise old bird who sits and rocks and ponders from his cabin perch.

Trait of a Good Man

Keep a man close who stays calm in times of adversity;
he'll be a good man in a storm.

ONE DOES NOT "BECOME" WISE

"Be sure to taste your words before you spit them out."
~ Gaelic Proverb

I had to laugh. Well, it was more of a chuckle.

You know, the kind of laughter when you have seen something so outrageous and over the top that you just have to grin and shake your head.

I had just opened an email from a young man who had worked for me until recently. I began to read what was the most hateful, vicious rant and diatribe imaginable. It was an insulting, verbal assault against me as a person and against my character.

IN SHORT, I AM HARD-PRESSED TO THINK OF ANOTHER TIME WHEN I HAVE BEEN SO MALIGNED AND DISRESPECTED. THE MAN WAS UNHINGED.

Having finished reading, I sat back and asked myself a question I have asked myself many times that follows along the line of the questions I shared in the pages at the front of this book: *what would be the wise response to this?*

The answer was obvious, of course. A wise man would NOT respond. What would have been the point? Again I chuckled and shook my head. I closed the email and moved on.

If I have learned anything through the years, it is that I am capable of being as big a fool as one can imagine, and at the same time, there is to be found in me a modicum of good sense—okay, wisdom.

This is true of all of us.

But, you don't just *become* wise.

It is against our nature. It is something you have to fight for.

Pride, ego, and various base emotions pull us toward the foolish. My lesser man wanted to respond to the young man in kind. But wisdom can only come from knowledge, understanding, self-control, and a conscious desire to rise above being a fool. It isn't easy to restrain yourself. If it was, we would all think and behave wisely.

Do for Yourself
and Others

Life isn't about weekends.
It's about being out there where you can make yourself useful.
Weekends should be earned.

PEARLS BEFORE SWINE

"Never teach a pig to sing.
It wastes your time and annoys the pig."
~Robert A. Heinlein
~ The Notebooks of Lazarus Long

When someone doesn't care what you think and disrespects you, it's best not to tell them what you think—even if they ask.

In other words, don't give something of value to those who do not appreciate its worth. That's the meaning of casting pearls before swine.

Life lessons learned the hard way are special treasures to an old man, to be shared only with people who can appreciate the worth of what you say.

Pay Attention, and Nobody Gets Hurt

There's always time to do things right the
first time and always time to do it SAFELY!
Nobody gets hurt, ya got that!?

THINKSPEAK

"All oppression creates a state of war."

~Simone de Beauvoir

Listen up, you astute sons and daughters of mothers. This is how I address the regular group of people I write for, and now, I am addressing you the same way.

When denied your right to think or speak, despotism is absolute. Think of this as one word: thinkspeak.

The point is that it is not possible to keep one from having their own thoughts, but when not free to express them, oppression is complete. At that juncture, the last vestige of freedom is taken from you.

Meanwhile, at Round Mountain, this was the subject of conversation at the RMCC (Round Mountain Critter Council) the other day. It was reaffirmed that all the critters would be free to have their own thoughts, to speak freely and that they would be valued for their individualism.

All right, enough of this. Go on now. I'm fixin' to go wanderin' about lookin' for dead trees, or ones that have fallen over, for next winter's firewood.

I ain't got no more time to be philosophizing.'

But do ponder on it, pilgrims.

Define Need

Frugality and simplicity in our lives seem
to be something of the distant past.

Boots

"You want to be happy?
You want to be well?
Then put your boots on."
~*Norah Vincent*

There is a time to put your boots on, and there is a time to take them off.

Know the difference. Learn to appreciate, and give thanks for both. You can see I just love wearing mine. Have for a real long time.

Little ol' me in my little ol' boots. Huh, I still dress the same way.

Don't Pee Up
a Flagpole, Either

I never get into a peeing contest with a skunk.

PUTTING TWO AND TWO TOGETHER

"My life had become a puzzle—its pieces
scattered about like paper in the wind,
with no one there to chase them but me."
~Meredith Taylor

Reaching a long-term goal is like working a jigsaw puzzle.

The desired result must be in clear focus. But you must also understand the value of finding two pieces that fit together.

My domestic critter, Leo, who insisted on adopting me years ago, giving me the bidness about reaching one of his long-term goals.

Why Do You Think We're Here?

A thoughtful man grows wise, over time,
from lessons learned being unwise.
If you go stupid, at least learn something.

WHAT'S ON YOUR MIND?

"I'm okay. Isn't that what I'm supposed to say?"

~Unknown

The above question is one we often hear as it falls within the context of "small talk."

"Howdy, how ya doin'?"

"I'm fine; how about you?"

"Oh, I'm fine, too. What's on your mind?"

"Nothing much."

I'm sure you can relate to being on both sides of this talk. You can also relate to the fact it is seldom true that we have nothing on our minds. Our minds are most often quite active. We're *always* thinking about something. The question is, *what?*

You can learn a great deal about yourself if you take time to note and think critically about what dominates your thoughts. Whether you are happy or miserable or have a positive or negative attitude about life, these thoughts, rooted inside your head, capture your mind.

WHAT CAPTURES YOUR MIND WILL CAPTURE YOUR HEART, AKA, WHAT YOU FEEL.

Consider this. If your heart is filled with hate, anger, rage, jealousy, envy, impatience, lust, greed, revenge, deceit, grief, worry, or false pride, there is no way you can be a happy, well-adjusted person capable of making wise decisions or playing a positive role in the lives of others.

If this is you, welcome to following the path of misery, foolishness, and self-destruction.

Conversely, if your mind is filled with love, joy, peace, contentment, faith, patience, humility, kindness, forgiveness, optimism, and generosity, you will find the key to being happy, well adjusted, and wise.

Wisdom comes from the heart.

It is evidence of a strong connection with our highest spiritual nature.

Foolishness comes when our hearts and minds give way to our baser nature.

Ponder on it, pilgrims.

Want the Simple Things

If you aren't content with what you have,
you most likely won't be content with more.
Learn to appreciate simple things.

HATERS LIVE RENT FREE

"Don't worry about those who talk behind your back.
They're behind you for a reason."
~Unknown

There's lots of talk these days about "haters."

Hate is a negative emotional state, closely akin to jealousy, that robs you of your individuality and gives someone else complete control over your life.

As they say, they live rent-free in your head.

The irony is you invite them in!

You've given them the power to take over your life, make you miserable, rob you of love, joy, happiness, and the ability to act rationally or reasonably.

Hate is a consuming fire that makes you crazy. I got no time for it.

Speaking of, I'm fixing to head up to Round Mountain. I need to get some chores done and check on my critters. I'll probably get in some rocking chair time, do some thinking, and maybe have a snort.

If it's been a tough week, stand tall because you hung tough and got the job done.

I'm proud of you.

Now, go have a week full of wonder and make some memories. It's much easier to do that with love in your heart—if you get my drift.

Resist the Temptation

Never corner something meaner than you are.

DEALING WITH RACIAL ISSUES IN THE WORKPLACE

"One day, our descendants will think it incredible that we paid so much attention to things like the amount of melanin in our skin or the shape of our eyes or our gender instead of the unique identities of each of us as complex human beings."
~Franklin A. Thomas

I

I posted a picture on LinkedIn with Arthur, aka Boobie, several months ago.

I spoke of the bond that has grown between us over the years he has been with me. I said that he had become like a son to me, which he has, and that he tells everyone I'm his daddy.

Though the resemblance is profound (grin), and that bond very real, it wasn't so in the beginning.

Boobie grew up in "The hood." Life was hard and tough. He tried to make it as best he could, in one way or the other.

I hired him because I thought he would be a good hand, maybe thinking he had something he wanted to prove and that he needed someone to believe in him.

Early on, in his first few days, he showed me he was a good worker.

I WAS A BIT FIRM WITH HIM AND GAVE HIM MOSTLY CRAPPY JOBS—THE "GOT GET THIS," "GO GET THAT" KIND. HECK, HE WAS THE NEW MAN AND HAD TO PAY SOME DUES.

But I started to sense what I felt was racial tension between us.

It wasn't coming from me, but him.

I was getting the impression he took me for "the big white bossman," who was treating him this way because he is a black man.

I decided to nip this in the bud and go over and hit him right between the eyes.

I have always believed the best way to deal with issues like this is head-on. So I walked over to Boobie, and the conversation went something like what follows:

"Boobie," I said.

"Yes, sir," he responded, turning to face me.

I paused, kind of looking around with a serious look on my face, then scratched my butt.

When I looked back at him, he was standing there peering into my face, obviously wondering what I wanted.

"Boobie," I said again. "Did you know white people like watermelon, too?"

THE LOOK ON HIS FACE WAS PRICELESS AND HARD TO DESCRIBE. THERE WAS SOME SHOCK IN IT FROM THE OUT-OF-THE-BLUE, OFF-THE-WALL OUTRAGEOUSNESS OF THE QUESTION. AND, I HAD SAID THE "W" WORD TO A BLACK MAN.

By today's politically correct standards, I should have been sent to Siberia, never to return, for daring to say such a profoundly "racist" thing. But there was also some quizzicalness on his face, like *what the "bleep" are you talking about?* I just stood there looking at him, grinning, waiting for his response.

He started laughing.

Boobie did respond to my question then, still laughing. He said, "And fried chicken?"

"Heck yes! Mashed taters, too."

"Green beans?" asked Boobie.

"Dang right, turnip greens."

"Oxtails?"

I said, "Oh Lord, everybody loves oxtails if you cook 'em right. I'll give you my recipe if you give me yours." Then I added, "White men like women awful well, too."

BOOBIE WAS LAUGHING SO HARD WITH GREAT BIG, DEEP BELLY ROARS THAT WITH HIS BOOMING VOICE, IT SOUNDED LIKE ROLLS OF THUNDER.

I stood there still, grinning at him as the "walls" crumbled before us, and things would never be the same.

Before I turned to walk away, I had one more thing to say in parting.

I faced him again and said to Boobie, "We're all just people, aren't we?"

As I walked away, I could still hear him laughing.

For the life of me, I cannot understand how this obvious truth is so difficult for some folks to understand.

Sure there are very superficial differences between people. We have different shades of skin, different colors of hair, and our eyes are not all shaped the same, but we're all just people.

It's something all of us need to realize.

"Jesus loves the little children, all the children of the world. Red and yellow, black and white, they are precious in His sight. Jesus loves the little children of the world." I learned this song in Sunday School when I was just a kid.

I like red and yellow, black, and white.

I like watermelon, too.

It's a Blessing

When someone underestimates you or takes you for a fool,
don't be angry. Grin, you own them.

MY FAVORITE QUESTION

"Choices are the hinges to destiny."
- Pythagoras

I sat across the lunch table from the president of a highly successful, multi-million-dollar company.

He was a younger man who was troubled and asking for my advice. I chuckled at myself with this thought that he wasn't as old as I was, but he wouldn't have noticed my inner mirth. Shucks, it seems everybody is younger than me nowadays. But actually, he was in his fifties.

One of his employees, a man who had been with him for years, and was like family, had committed an egregious act of poor judgment. The potential ramifications seemed endless. His entire business family was upset and watching to see how he would deal with it.

Doing nothing was not an option in this case.

He sat there explaining to me what the man had done, how it had affected other employees, and the potential consequences that could reach the point of legal action being taken against his business.

His facial expressions revealed stress, frustration, a touch of anger, and hurt.

Then he asked me, "What do you think I should do?"

I hesitated for a moment, just to make him think I was ponderin' on his question when I had already decided on my response as he was telling me the story, should he ask me.

This wasn't my first rodeo.

I answered his question with a question, "What would a wise man do?"

What I saw as I watched him was predictable. His demeanor changed, and his facial expressions immediately gave way to becoming calm, serious, and thoughtful. Where I had seen anxiety, I now saw studious consideration.

I sat silently and waited for him to speak.

He began articulating some thoughts, thinking out loud, so to speak. I listened, feeling it best not to respond for the moment. Eventually, he settled on two possible courses of action then asked me my opinion.

I replied, "Both seem good. Which do you think would be best for your business and all concerned?"

He thought for a moment and said, "The first one."

I have observed over the years that there is something therapeutic in simply asking this question. I see it in my own life and in others when I ask them. As a person is ponderin' it, stress and anxiety give way to a proactive mindset focused on making the best decision possible—being wise. Foraging for this answer takes you beyond reacting emotionally, in the heat of the moment, to a studied, measured solution.

"What would a wise person do?"

"What would a wise person say?"

When making decisions and advising others, ask yourself these questions (and the other two of the Four Golden Questions I laid out for you at the beginning of this book). Just keep in mind that the best answer might often be, "Nothing."

Ponder on it, pilgrims.

Just Two Kinds

The way I see it, there are just two kinds of people
in this world. Folks who hunt and fish,
and folks who kill and catch.

THELMA'S WORK-LIFE BALANCE

"Keep busy at something;
a busy person never had time to be unhappy."
~Robert Louis Stevenson

As you know, Thelma is the enforcer of the Round Mountain Critter Code of Conduct. (RMCCC).

She runs a tight ship, trust me.

But even Thelma has her lighter moments. This week, she was playing peek-a-boo with Rocko, also a Round Mountain legend, as you know, and one handsome raccoon. Both were having a great time. It's okay to get a little silly once in a while. It keeps you young.

I'm fixing to head up the Carefree Highway to check on my critters and give some belly rubs. So go on now, git on outta here. I've had a belly full of ya this week.

BEING A WORK HORSE

"Earning Your Keep"

THE RED LETTER DAYS OF LIFE

"Pain is weakness leaving the body."
- United States Marine Corps

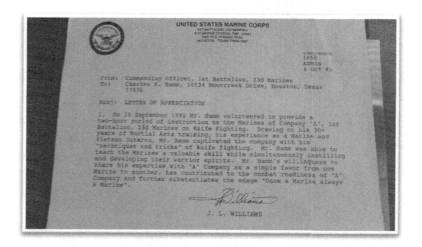

As we travel along the twists and turns of the road of life, there are certain days that, for one reason or another, make a memory we never forget.

They roll around each year, and our minds are taken back once again as we relive that special moment in time.

On 18 April 1969, I was honorably discharged from the United States Marine Corps. This is a day of significance in my life. Naturally, I always remember 17 June 1965, which was the day I arrived at MCRD (Marine Corps Recruit Depot) in San Diego when my four-year journey began.

I DIDN'T CELEBRATE THAT DATE THEN, NOR DO I NOW. IT IS A DAY OF REFLECTION, SOBRIETY, AND A STORM OF MEMORIES THAT SWIRL THROUGH MY MIND.

Some of the memories I have spent a lifetime trying to forget. In ways I understand and ways I am sure I don't understand, those four years of my young life defined me and changed me forever.

I would never be the same.

I became a Marine, and you can't un-become a Marine.

It's forever.

Another red-letter day in my life was the honor of being invited to give some training to the young Marines who shared this leg of my journey. I remember so many of their faces.

I have often reflected on that day and feel certain some of those Marines in attendance went on to war. Did I play any part in helping them do their duty, accomplish their mission, and survive? I want to think so.

This year, around that date, I'm taking off Friday to have a three-day weekend at Round Mountain. I know my critters will be lined up on the porch of the cabin to get their belly rubs. I intend to get in some rocking chair time, think about some stuff, toast the Corps and my Marine brothers of all generations.

Now, I can't talk about this anymore. It's making my tattoo itch.

It's Tricky

Wisdom is born of knowledge and experience.
However, knowledge and experience will
not necessarily make one wise.

HORSEPOWER

*"I found the key to the universe
in the engine of an old, parked car."*
~ *Bruce Springsteen*

What would be your definition of a good vehicle?
Mine is simple: does it start, and does it go?

THE ODOMETER ON MY FJ CRUISER ROLLED OVER TO 400,000 MILES YESTERDAY.

It still starts, and it still goes. I have no intention of trading it until it rolls over and dies.

Many people seem to think their vehicle defines them. In one sense of the word, old "FJ" defines me as well.

I have never cared what people think of my success, or lack thereof, financially. I believe many people buy the most expensive vehicle they can afford to make payments on, and although people might think they are prosperous, the fact is that vehicle payments are far too often a crushing burden to your personal finances. I'd rather have a few bucks in my pocket and have people think I'm poor than have people think I'm prosperous—when I'm really broke.

I never buy something I don't need.

So even though FJ has racked up quite a few miles—knocking on the door of half a million—do I need a new work vehicle?

Shucks, no!

FJ and I have been through a lot together and made many memories. It's a keeper. I'm looking forward to 500,000 miles.

It still starts and goes every morning. That's the only truth I need to know to make my decision.

A Modicum of Control

You can't keep negative, toxic, angry, offensive,
or insulting people out of your life.
But you can keep them out of your head.

WOULD YOU LIKE TO BE RICH?

"Being rich is having money.
Being wealthy is having time."
~Stephen Swid

Would you like to be rich?

**BEFORE YOU ANSWER THAT QUESTION, ANSWER THIS
ONE: HOW WOULD YOU DEFINE BEING RICH?**

The concept is relative.

If you make $50,000 a year, and your living expenses keep you in constant financial stress, you probably think someone who makes $100,000 a year is rich.

Would it surprise you to know that this person feels the same strain? They probably think someone making $200,000 a year has it made.

And so it goes.

It has been my experience, antidotal for sure, that all of the above would be wrong.

We live in a culture that encourages spending and the accumulation of stuff. People, regardless of how much they make, so often will live to the very extent of their means. When the bills are paid, they have nothing left over.

Such people will never "get ahead."

**PROSPERITY BEGINS WITH SAVING MONEY.
THIS IS A HABIT THAT FEW HAVE.**

I'm not talking about saving so you can buy something. I'm talking about socking away cash and not touching it for any reason. Leave it alone and let it build.

If you are not a saver, start now, and start small if you must, but retire some money. Then get in the habit of saving.

Some of what you make should be yours, of course. But I think you will be amazed at how even a modest effort will build up over time. As it does, your spirits will rise, as will your options. Feed the piggy.

You Can Do It!

Often in life, decisions are basic.
Like, can I take one more step?
We always have one more step in us.
Keep going.

TAKING YOUR LIFE
TO THE NEXT LEVEL

"You must learn a new way to think
before you can master a new way to be."
~ Unknown

Learning to appreciate, and being content with your life, in the "now" is a wonderful way to live.

Some really special, unexpected events often happen along the path of each given day. However, our minds can become so cluttered that we can fail to notice the moment-to-moment changes and blessings for which we should be grateful—for the joy we could know at the time.

THIS IS NOT TO SAY THAT NO THOUGHT SHOULD BE GIVEN FOR TOMORROW. A LIFE WELL LIVED MUST HAVE SOME PLANNING IF YOUR DREAMS ARE TO COME TRUE.

Each day can be filled with joy, excitement and recognized as a segment of a journey that is taking you where you want to go.

So many people I know have no shortage of dreams, but they are fuzzy, vague, and seem to lack one essential quality that gives them any chance of success. SELF DISCIPLINE.

Self-discipline will take your life to a higher, more meaningful level.

It is self-control.

It is self-restraint.

It is willingly deferring the temptations of the "now" for what is more important to you.

It is a choice YOU make, not imposed on you.

It is you taking charge of your own life.

Give some thought to where you want life to take you. Enjoy each day, but know that tomorrow will come. Don't let life be something that happens to you. Take it by the horns and rein yourself in.

Living in the now must not mean squandering away tomorrow.

Another Golden Rule

Put your Wranglers on before your boots.

NEVER SPEND IT ALL

"Don't go broke trying to look rich.
Act your wage!"
~ Unknown

Frugality and simplicity in our lives seem like they are in the distant past nowadays.

As I got on about in the last couple of pages, rather than having a few bucks in their pocket, folks would rather have people *think* that they do.

Changing this may sound ridiculously simple, but the more you think about it, the more profound it becomes.

My personal economic plan is both simple and profound. It's also worked for me for decades: "NEVER SPEND IT ALL."

Heck, I don't claim to be an expert, but when a way of life works, you want to share it. Try it and see if you can't get ahead just a titch.

And I Don't Want To

I always see people staring at their phones,
so I thought I'd try it. I don't get it.

Until It's Time to Pee on the Fire

"I may not be the strongest.
I may not be the fastest.
But I'll be damned if I'm not trying my hardest."
~ Unknown

Sometimes the going gets a might tough. You can whine and moan all you want, but things still have to get done.

Be grateful for your job.

Have resolve.

Get your mind right.

Have some fun.

I expect your best effort until it's time to pee on the fire and call in the dogs come supper time Friday evening.

Through a Particular Lens

Our strength can be our weakness, and our weakness
can be our strength. It's all in how you look at it.

ARE YOU A LEADER?

"To handle yourself, use your head.
To handle others, use your heart."
~Eleanor Roosevelt

A lot of folks write and talk about leadership these days. The way I see it, a leader leads: he is someone people follow. If you want to know if you're a leader, get to the job site, get out of your truck, and get after it. Every now and then, look back and see if anyone is behind you.

You are
Someone Special

Develop and maximize your gifts without comparing
yourself to others or trying to be someone else.

A Job Well Done

"Most people work at keeping their job, rather than doing a good job. If you're the former, you're leading a meaningless life. If you're the latter, keep up the good work."
- George Lois

Work is a wonderful opportunity to provide service to our fellow man, as well as prosper individually and enjoy a good life.

I have always loved the feeling that comes from a job well done.

Be blessed as you bless others.

It Works Better Like That

Keep your head screwed on straight.

THE REPUBLIC OF
ROUND MOUNTAIN

"Animals are inspirational.
They don't know how to lie.
They are natural forces."
~Charles Bukowski

Meanwhile, in The Republic of Round Mountain, all is well.

Our plan for national defense is sound, and all the critters are calm, cool, and resolved. I canceled the daily training schedule and declared Saturday "Belly Rub Day" to keep morale up.

In this picture, Spuds is leading a contingent of the wild hog infantry down to the cabin to get their turn. They do love their belly rubs. At the end of the day, I was plumb wore out.

Now, I'm fixing to get in some back porch rockin' chair time. Might have a smoke and a snort, come to think of it, and do some thinkin'. Y'all are a distraction and are startin' to wear on me. Best toddle off now.

This Will Make
You Feel Better

Freedom cannot be lost.
It must be surrendered.

THE CRITTERS CHOOSE
INDEPENDENCE AND FREEDOM

"Freedom is the open window through which pours the sunlight of the human spirit and human dignity."
~ *Herbert Hoover*

By unanimous vote, the critters of Round Mountain chose independence and freedom at this morning's meeting of the RMCC.

In addition, by unanimous vote, we agreed we would make our stand here on Round Mountain.

We will live free or die.

We pledged to defend Round Mountain against all enemies, foreign and domestic, of our Constitution and our Constitutional Republic – whatever the cost.

This ain't no place for the timid soul.

Such folks won't have our backs when it's nut cuttin' time anyway.

Remember that.

Git It Straight!

Ponder about what's really important.

Round Mountain
Infantry Battalion

*"If we come to a minefield, our infantry
attacks exactly as if it were not there."*
~ *Georgy Zhukov*

Thelma and I had a special meeting after the regular meeting of the RMCC to discuss who would head up the RMIB (Round Mountain Infantry Battalion).

WE AGREED THAT THE INFANTRY SHOULD CONSIST OF PROFANE, UNRULY, OBNOXIOUS, CERTIFIABLY CRAZY, OCCASIONAL BRAWLERS, WITH TOTAL DISREGARD FOR THEIR PERSONAL SAFETY.

The leader must be totally devoted to the mission regardless of cost, and above all, have a pair.

Although Thelma and Spuds have had issues in the past, she had to agree that Spuds, leading a pack of wild hogs, filled the bill.

Now, he will now lead the "balls out" Round Mountain Infantry charge when we commit it to action. Here's a picture of his backside, so you know what I mean and that he's fit for the job.

Now, I got plans to make. I'm fixing to head out on my first trip since I retired to check out some archeological sites of interest and some family history.

Thelma will head things up at Round Mountain while I'm gone and make sure the training schedule is followed to the letter.

Don't even think about snooping around here. It won't end well for ya.

But I still love y'all. Ya know, in case ya forgot.

We Strike at Midnight!

Let's start a grassroots wildfire that will lead
to a revival of common sense, and wisdom,
in a world that seems to have forsaken both.

THE DEFENSE OF ROUND MOUNTAIN

"He could tell by the way the animals walked that they were keeping time to some kind of music. Maybe it was the song in their own hearts that they walked to."
~ Laura Adams Armer

An update: the various critter clans are choosing their leaders, and I will be meeting with them to discuss the defense of Round Mountain now that it has been declared a 2A Sanctuary.

I, of course, will be the supreme commander, with Thelma second in command.

Every critter on Round Mountain will be called on to serve. I hope they are ready and that they took their training seriously. What's going down around here is no joke.

That's all I can share today as I got places to go and stuff to do, and you ain't comin'.

REFLECTIONS ON A LIFE

"Looking Back"

If That Ol' Sycamore
Could Talk

"Stars shining bright above you.
Night breezes seem to whisper 'I love you."
Birds singing in the sycamore tree.
Dream a little dream of me."
~ "Dream a Little Dream of Me,"
Wilbur Schwandt, George Kahn, Fabian Andre

The two fishermen anchored their boat not far off the shore from where I stood.

I have seen them here every week for a number of years.

One was an older man, and the other younger, middle-aged. I knew they were father and son from listening to their conversations as they fished. I looked forward to seeing them each week. They seemed to always take note of me each time they came. One day I overheard the following conversation:

"You know, if that ol' sycamore could talk, he could tell some tales," said the father to the son as they both looked at me.

"Bet he could," replied the son, smiling.

The two men had no idea, but I did have a tale to tell, and it was about them.

OF COURSE, AT THE TIME, THIRTY YEARS AGO, THE WHOLE STORY COULD ONLY PARTIALLY BE TOLD. NOW, ALL THESE YEARS LATER, IT IS STILL UNFOLDING.

It is a story of the love the two men obviously felt for each other and the special time they shared each week out here fishing. But, like so many stories do, it turned into one of great sorrow, and at times, it broke my heart.

Although I couldn't have known it at the time, the day I spoke of in the beginning was the last time I would ever see them out here fishing together.

Their story would continue, but it took a heart-wrenching turn.

I don't remember when it hit me. But I did notice the following week that they did not come to fish.

I didn't think much about it. Occasionally they would miss a week. Then the weeks turned into months, and at some point, I wondered if something had happened.

I was sad and missed seeing them.

TIME MARCHED ON. MY LEAVES FELL, REAPPEARED, AND STARTED TO TURN THEIR FALL COLORS AGAIN. IT HAD NOW BEEN ABOUT A YEAR SINCE I HAD SEEN THEM.

I remembered that my leaves had only started to turn the last time they were here. Orion was now back in the early morning sky, as it had been on what I hadn't known would be their final fishing trip.

Then one day, I noticed a vehicle pull over to the side of the road behind me, and a man emerged. I didn't pay much attention at first. I thought he was just another fisherman who would come down to fish off the bank.

Yet he didn't have fishing tackle with him, and he wasn't dressed like someone who intended to spend the day fishing. I paid closer attention.

His behavior was very strange. He was a slim, fit man dressed in Western attire, and I didn't expect to see such a man crying, but he did. Although "crying" is not the best choice of a word. The man was overcome with grief. He looked about aimlessly for a moment, then walked down the bank toward the water where a large cluster of goldenrod was in full bloom. He pulled out a pocket knife and cut a large bouquet of wildflowers, then trudged back up to the road. From there, he walked out onto the bridge, where I was standing to the left of him, and he looked out at the water.

I was alarmed, thinking he was going to jump off the bridge.

But he didn't. Instead, he spoke, directing his words as if to someone down on the water. He was so distraught that it was hard to understand what he was saying. After several minutes he leaned over the bridge railing, dropped the bouquet of flowers into the water, and watched them float away on the current.

To my surprise, he then looked up at me and spoke, "Morning, Mr. Sycamore. If you could talk, I'll bet you could tell some tales." Saying this seemed to intensify his grief, and he turned back to the water, sobbing.

It was at this moment I realized who he was.

When I saw his face, as he peered up at me, I thought I knew, but when he said what he did, I had no doubt.

He was the younger man who had once come to this spot weekly to fish with his father. His behavior that morning told me why they had stopped coming. It had to be that the older man had died. It all made sense to me now.

The man walked back to his vehicle, stopping once to gaze back at me, and then he did something I didn't expect. He saluted me. After that, he hurried back to his car and drove away. I knew I would never see him again. But I had the end of the story that I had wondered about that whole past year.

Or did I?

My leaves once again fell, winter came, then spring and summer. I thought of the man and his father from time to time. The memory of the grieving son made an impression I knew I would not forget. That's when I noticed my leaves starting to change again, and Orion was back. It had been another year since the day the son had been here.

To my surprise, I watched as the same vehicle drove up and parked. A man got out, and it was him—like he was on cue. As if he had marked the date to return. For the second straight year, still overcome with grief, the man followed the same routine as the year before. He cut flowers, walked to the bridge, spoke out to the water, dropped the bouquet, and spoke to me. Walking back, he turned and saluted me before he drove off. I was astonished.

HE CAME BACK ON THE THIRD YEAR, THE FOURTH, THE FIFTH, AND SO ON....

It has now been thirty years since the young man fished here with his father. He has come every year at the same time, cut flowers, walked onto the bridge, spoke out to the water, and talked to and saluted me before driving away.

I realized years ago that each time he spoke out to the water, he had been talking to his father, telling him of the events of the past year. He hasn't missed a year.

Some things have changed.

On the seventh year, he followed his ritual without crying.

Then an irony to the story crept in. I noticed as the years went by, he aged. Today, as he stood there on the bridge, he wasn't a young man any longer. He looked the age I remembered his father to be—maybe even a might older.

I HAVE TO ADMIT, I WAS THE ONE SHEDDING A TEAR THEN.

Time marches on, and I know the year will come that will be his last. He will have gone on to be with his father, and I will never see him again. Until then, I will cherish each year because I know he will come. When he doesn't anymore, I will grieve, but I will also rejoice at the thought of him being with his father on another shore, where they can fish together again.

Perhaps a sycamore tree will be rooted there that can continue their story, which will go on for eternity. Perhaps it will be me.

Yes, I do have some tales to tell, as I remain embedded in the Earth, overseeing people coming and going, some staying longer than others, some never returning. I can't say that the son, standing on the bridge now, has told anyone about his annual pilgrimage, probably not. But I know, and now, you do, too.

***

The last time Daddy and I went fishing before he died, he made the comment to me, "If that ol' sycamore tree could talk, he could tell some tales." That gave me the idea to write the story from its perspective.

Nothing in life quite compares to the loss of a loved one. We go through the process of grieving, but in time, that gives way to memories and the legacy they left behind.

We have different ways of dealing with grief but also different ways of remembering. We remember their birthday, but also the day they died. There are special places where we feel connected with them. For me, it was where my daddy and I would fish. With many, it is the graves. Perhaps, for some, not all memories are good ones, but we must remember all of us are flawed.

Most importantly, we must give them honor. Departed loved ones touched our lives and had a part in molding us into the person we have become. My annual pilgrimage to the lake is to honor my father and show my respects.

Find your touchstone with the people you have lost in your life. It is the proper thing to do and good for the soul.

Last picture with my daddy, October 17, 1990.

Open Your Eyes

If you can't even entertain the idea that you might be part of the problem, you will never see anything clearly.

SETTING SAIL FOR OKINAWA

"Not a tourist. I live here." - Words written on an American soldier's helmet in Vietnam

As a nineteen-year-old Marine, I boarded the *USS St. Clair County* in San Diego and headed west. It was 15 January 1966, over a half-decade ago. It took us thirty-one days, as I recall, to get to Okinawa, where we would undergo more training and then head to Vietnam.

The ship was an LST (Landing Ship, Tank), which has a flat bottom for beach landings. It was quite a ride, and I made memories that have lasted a lifetime.

That's my 1096 ship in the background.
Courtesy of Wikipedia.

**THIS WAS THE BEGINNING OF A TIME IN
MY LIFE THAT WOULD CHANGE ME FOREVER.
NOTHING WOULD EVER BE QUITE THE SAME.**

Semper Fidelis Marines, and God bless those wonderful sailors who served on the LSTs. Tough duty.

If It's Not Fine,
It's Not Over

Give thanks, have hope, and be of good cheer.
Everthang is going to be just fine.

OLD FASHIONED FATHERS

"A son's first hero is his dad."
~ Unknown (but true)

I remember how nervous I felt, fixing to do something I had never done: defy my father.

Daddy had rules when I was growing up, and I was about to break two of the big ones. He always said I could not smoke or drink coffee until I was a man, and this morning I intended to do both when I sat down with him at the kitchen table at just nineteen years old.

I started smoking and drinking coffee in Marine Corps Boot Camp. (I quit smoking when I was thirty years old.)

After boot camp and basic infantry training, I went home for my first leave.

I felt like a man now. The Marine Corps seemed to think so, but I had to establish that with my father. His opinion was most important to me.

WHEN I AWOKE MY FIRST MORNING HOME, I WALKED INTO THE KITCHEN, AND DADDY SAT THERE HAVING COFFEE AND SMOKING A CIGARETTE.

I wished him good morning and walked over and poured myself a cup of coffee. He watched me without expression. I then reached into my pocket and pulled out my cigarettes, lit one, and looked him straight in the eyes.

An almost imperceptible grin came to the corners of his mouth, but he never said a word. It was at this moment in time that I first, truly, felt like a man. Tacitly, Daddy had tipped his hat to me with his silence, and things would never be the same. At that moment, Daddy and I became equals, men and best friends.

Growing up, Daddy was not my friend. He was my father, a loving and gentle man but strict. He was consistent and fair and never raised his voice but spoke firmly. We never wrestled on the floor, acted silly, or played and joked around. Daddy took me hunting and fishing with him, taught me to love the forest creatures, and to know their habits. He taught me the names of the different trees, marksmanship, and firearm safety. But, he always maintained a "presence" and a certain distance. It seemed that he had some sense that he had this little boy to raise, who would so soon be grown and gone, so he needed to teach me some things. Daddy was my mentor, always teaching.

Things He Taught Me

- ❖ Don't talk with food in your mouth.
- ❖ Don't put your elbows on the table.
- ❖ Say, "Please, and thank you."
- ❖ Say, "Yes sir and no sir, yes ma'am and no ma'am."
- ❖ Open the door for ladies and let them walk in first.
- ❖ Treat everyone with respect.
- ❖ If a lady drops something, pick it up for her.
- ❖ Stand up when a lady enters the room and offer her your seat.
- ❖ Don't interrupt adult conversation.
- ❖ Never back down to a bully.
- ❖ Be thankful for work.
- ❖ Be honest in dealing with others.
- ❖ Always tell the truth.
- ❖ Never spend all your money.
- ❖ Don't say" bad words" in the presence of ladies.

I could go on and on. Being proper and having good manners was important to him. I always knew exactly where I stood, and there was no confusion about it. If I behaved properly, all was well. There was a certain sense of security and stability in knowing where I stood and that how my day would go was within my control.

BUT, AS I HAVE MUSED ABOUT DADDY MORE THAN USUAL THESE PAST SEVERAL DAYS, THERE IS ONE LESSON I LEARNED FROM HIM THAT HE NEVER ONCE MENTIONED: AUTHORITY.

Daddy was an authority figure in my young life, and his rules were my laws. There would be consequences for disobedience: his "look" of displeasure, a warning, and, yes, an occasional spanking. His authority has been a lesson that has served me well as an adult.

When I observe young families today, so often, the father seems to try to be a buddy or friend to their sons. That comes later. As children are growing up, they need a FATHER. Trying to be both only creates uncertainty and confusion in the mind of a child.

My daddy was born one hundred years ago, 20 February 1918. I lost him in 1990, but he has lived on in my heart and soul each day.

Happy birthday, Daddy. You were a great, old-fashioned father.

For that, I'm thankful.

You Will Value
This a Little Later

Life lessons learned the hard way are special treasures
to an old man, to be shared with the worthy.

Marching Out of Step

"So much of who we are is where we have been."
~ William Langewiesche

I remember getting off the plane.

I don't really know what I was thinking or expecting. For thirteen months, I had been out of the country, and now I felt torn. A part of me wanted to get on the next plane for the last leg of my journey, which would take me home. Another part wanted to get on a plane and go back where I had been.

As I walked through the airport, I was ignored.

That didn't really matter to me. In fact, I felt a might relieved as I had heard stories of some who were less fortunate.

I walked into a bar and was hoping that being in uniform, I could buy a beer without being carded. After all, I was only twenty years old. Then I noticed what was on TV.

Hordes of angry young people were screaming in the streets, chanting, "Hell no, we won't go." Someone got up to address the crowd and launched into a tirade about the atrocities of the American military in that far-off land I had only left two days before. An American flag burned, and to my further amazement, the flag I had been told was the ensign of the "bad guys" was waved about.

I looked around the bar, still ignored.

I forgot about the beer and walked back outside. It seemed that the United States was a different world than the one I had left. The folks on TV were focused on what all was wrong with our country, and I was a big part of it.

Through the years, not much has changed.

When I turn on the news these days, it seems that I am still the quintessential representative of everything that is wrong with our country. The list of names being thrown about to describe me range from "Nazi" and "racist" to a man who hates women and children. Apparently, my heart is dark, sinister, and filled with hate. I'm "deplorable," I'm told, and look, I have a rifle! So I represent the "stupidity" of the American people, and you can smell me all over the Wal-Mart.

I AM ALSO A MAN POSSESSED WITH ANY NUMBER OF "PHOBIAS." I'M A THISOPHOBE, A THATOPHOBE, AND A THEOTHEROPHOBE. I COULD GO ON.

While rockin' on the porch of my cabin at Round Mountain last weekend, I thought of more phobias that I don't hear much about from the people who never tire of shooting me the bird. You won't find these words in a dictionary since I just made them up. And since I coined the words, I get the right to define them. None describe me.

Here are four new phobias:

Libertasophobe: These are people who fear and/or despise freedom and liberty. They live in freedom and liberty and use its opportunities to oppose it. I am a man who wants to live my own life and take responsibility for myself. This is the essence of freedom. I ask for nothing and expect nothing but the right to "take my own chances, and pay my own dues." I make my own way, accept the consequences of my own decisions, and fight my own demons alone.

Opusophobe: These are people who fear and/or despise work. It seems that the folks out to change the world, save the planet, and turn our country upside down have little interest in finding a meaningful way of being of service to their fellow man, but this is the definition of work.

They are content to let others provide for them, thinking those who do work owe them something. I don't owe them anything. Helping someone is not giving them something. It is teaching them to help themselves. Folks seem to get that mixed up.

Cogitareophobe: These are people who fear and/or despise thinking their own thoughts. They actually promote an environment where "group think" is the norm and despise those who disagree with them. They seem incapable of having one thought that is not permitted by their masters, who have stuffed them all into a tiny box, and worry about what will happen to them should they choose to think their own thoughts. They never seem to realize that with the passing of time, they just might see some things differently.

**NOTHING IS MORE SACRED THAN OUR RIGHT
TO DO OUR OWN THINKING, HAVE OUR OWN
OPINIONS, AND THE RIGHT TO SPEAK OUR MINDS.
I HAVE RESISTED INDOCTRINATION SINCE I WAS A BOY.**

I once told a preacher, who had become quite upset with me because I was straying from "the truth," that if I went to hell over a doctrinal error in scripture, it would be my error and not his.

Auctoritatisophobe: These are people who fear and/or despise authority. The irony here is they lash out at those who have rightful authority to maintain order, and civility in society, while seeking, at the same time, an all-powerful governmental system that will exercise absolute authority over them and tolerate no dissent.

If history teaches one lesson, it is that when a government becomes all-powerful, scoundrels and tyrants take charge. It never works out well for the people.

Such were my musings as I snorted a bit of Jack and gave belly rubs to the critters who came by to visit me on the porch. The critters like me. It's a good thing I like them, too.

Don't Be Full of Horse Pucky

If you say you believe in something and then go all to pieces when your faith is challenged, you really don't believe at all.

MY SEARCH FOR
JOHN AND ALEX

*"A true soldier fights not because he hates what's in front
of him, but because he loves what is behind him."*
~ Unknown

The two young men grew up and came of age in remote, deep rural areas in Nicholas County, Kentucky.

Their homesteads were many miles apart. Perhaps they knew each other, I can't really say, but they probably weren't friends.

John was six years older than Alex, which is quite an age spread when you're young, so there would not have been much contact between them. John was born on 11 July 1837, and Alex on 18 October 1843.

HOWEVER, THEY DID HAVE ONE THING IN COMMON.
BOTH HAD HEARD THE DISTANT DRUMS OF WAR,
AND BOTH HAD ANSWERED THE CALL.

John enlisted in the 4th Kentucky Calvary and Alex with the 3rd Kentucky Calvary. The American Civil War had called them both to the service of their country. Their paths crossed on several occasions in minor actions, but both fought in the desperate Battle of Atlanta.

Just one distinction adds a certain twist to the story. John fought for the Union and Alex for the Confederacy. They both survived the war, came back to Nicholas County, and married and fathered children. I know this because their stories and lives are particularly meaningful to me.

HAD EITHER FALLEN IN THAT WAR, I WOULD NOT EXIST. THEY ARE BOTH BLOOD, AND THE BOND OF BLOOD HAS ALWAYS COURSED STRONGLY THROUGH MY VEINS.

You see, John Robert Dayton was my great-great-grandfather on my mother's side of the family, and Alexander Kimes Hamm was my great grandfather on my daddy's side.

Paying a visit to John Robert Dayton

I had just returned, after being gone for a spell, from my first "retirement adventure," a quest to find the graves of both of these men, so I could show my respects.

MANY PLACES ARE ON MY RETIRED BUCKET LIST. THEY EVEN INCLUDE ANCIENT RUINS FROM THE FAR CORNERS OF THE EARTH. BUT NOTHING WAS MORE IMPORTANT TO ME THAN HONORING THESE MEN.

In rural America, back in these times, cemeteries were often no more than family plots, where family members and close neighbors would be buried. They are scattered about the countryside, and many are lost to the memories of people—even direct descendants—who now live in those areas. Time has passed them by.

Another issue, in my quest, was that no one had been buried in these cemeteries for a hundred years or more.

Nature had taken its course. Trees, briars, and other forest vegetation reclaimed the stones. These are not manicured cemeteries; no, they are lost, forgotten, and swallowed up by the march of time.

From research I had done before my journey began, I thought I knew the general area where I might find both graves.

The problem was to actually find the cemetery and then, which proved to be equally difficult, to find the graves. Many of the grave markers were nothing but small blank stones; some had writing but were so worn I could not make out the words. I did find, I am absolutely sure, the cemetery where Alexander is buried.

I remembered my daddy telling me, many years ago, that he was buried in a small cemetery up on a hill behind the old schoolhouse in Ellisville, Kentucky, where Daddy was born and raised. So, I hiked up there and found an old cemetery. It was little more than a thicket with a few stones scattered about.

I walked where I could and crawled where I couldn't for several hours. I knew Alexander was there, but his actual grave is now known only to God. I did not find his grave and was deeply disappointed. Still, I knew in my heart; I had done all I could to find him.

I paused before leaving, took off my hat, placed it over my heart, and spoke a few words to him. Then, I put my hat back on, snapped my heels together, and saluted smartly, stating. "Respect, soldier! Your blood flows in me; you're family. You are not forgotten."

Now it was time to see if I could find John Robert. I figured finding the cemetery where Alex was buried would be easier than finding his marker, and I was right. There was no point of reference like, "Up on the hill behind the old schoolhouse."

I only knew the general area where the Dayton family lived at that time. I'll spare you a lot of the details, but after quite a hike and a lot of roaming around, I found a cemetery back in a woody lot surrounded by hay fields. I wasn't sure he was buried there but began a thorough search, on my feet when I could and my hands and knees when I had to.

To my amazement, after about twenty minutes of looking at the few surviving headstones that seemed to be scattered about with no clear pattern, I walked up to a stone that seemed well preserved. It wasn't him, but I noticed that on the other side of the large blue ash tree behind this stone was another gravestone.

Tree limbs were low, and the ubiquitous briars made it hard to get to, but I crawled toward it. When I looked up, I saw the name "Dayton." My heart leaped in my chest as I looked more closely.

IT READ, "JOHN R. DAYTON.
BORN JULY 11, 1837, DIED JULY 27, 1878.
IT WAS HIM.
I HAD FOUND MY GREAT-GREAT-GRANDFATHER.

I sat there, transfixed on the ground before it, and then noticed another gravestone right behind his. Though difficult, I could read it. "William G. Dayton." This was John Robert's father, my great-great-great-grandfather!

I was astounded, to say the least, and got a might emotional. *Blood! Their blood is my blood. They live on in me.*

There is something I haven't told you about John Robert. He had survived the war, only to be murdered in Mount Olivet, Kentucky, at the age of forty-one years old. That was all I knew as I laid eyes on his stone. It touches my heart that he is buried next to his father.

I made mention of my adventure on LinkedIn, and the wife of one of my contacts, a Mrs. Debbie Taft, researched and found the newspaper article giving the account of John Robert's tragic death. Thank you, Ms. Debbie. You solved a family mystery for me, and I can rest a little easier.

Here's a photocopy of the article and the wording used to explain what happened to my great-great-grandfather.

ROBERTSON COUNTY.

A Band of Regulators Commit a Cowardly Murder and Burn a House —Three Persons Arrested on Suspicion.

[Special Dispatch to the Courier-Journal.]

MAYSVILLE, July 29.—On Saturday night, between midnight and one o'clock, a band of the so-called regulators of Robertson county, some twenty-five or thirty in number, visited the premises of John Dayton, a respectable farmer living near Mt. Olivet, for the purpose, it is reported, of settling a difficulty said to exist in his family. On reaching the door of his dwelling they demanded to see Dayton, but, having heard them as they entered his premises, he endeavored to escape through the back yard. Mrs. Dayton, in order to delay the regulators so as to favor her husband's escape, spoke to them and told them Mr. Dayton was not at home. She had hardly ceased speaking when six or seven shots were heard in the rear of the house. The regulators had discovered him, and fired as he was in the act of getting over a fence. He dropped to the ground and died instantly, the ball having entered his back and passed out through his heart. Leaving the Dayton farm, the band went to a tenement house belonging to Avis Throckmorton, and burned it. It was to have been occupied to-day by R. Hanson, who was at the time Marshal of Mt. Olivet, and as an officer had arrested some of the regulators for disorderly conduct about a month ago. Dayton had a difficulty with William Claypole, who is believed to be a regulator, about a hog. It is said Claypole last Saturday, while drunk at Mt. Olivet, said, "We are going to settle with Dayton to-night, and he will never make another settlement." Claypole, Henry Rankins and Alfred Murray have been arrested on suspicion. They are now in jail at Mt. Olivet. Dayton was about 40 years old and in good circumstances. He leaves a wife and six children. There is a good deal of excitement over the affair in Robertson.

Robertson County.

A Band of Regulators Commit a Cowardly Murder and
Burn a House—Three Persons Arrested on Suspicion

(Special Dispatch to the Courier-Journal.)

Maysville, July 29. – On Saturday night, between midnight and one o'clock, a band of so-called regulators of
Robertson county, some twenty-five or thirty in number, visited the premises of John Dayton, a
respectable farmer living near Mt. Olivet, for the
purpose, it is reported, of settling a difficulty said to
exist in his family. On reaching the door of his dwelling
they demanded to see Dayton, but, having heard them
as they entered his premise, he endeavored to escape
through the backyard. Mrs. Dayton, in order to delay
the regulators so as to favor her husband's escape,
spoke to them and told them Mr. Dayton was not at
home. She had hardly ceased speaking when six or
seven shots were heard in the rear of the house. The
regulators had discovered him, and fired as he was in
the act of getting over a fence. He dropped to the
ground and died instantly, the ball having entered his
back and passed out through his heart. Leaving the
Dayton farm, the band went to a tenement house
belonging to Avis Throckmorton, and burned it. It was
to have been occupied to-day by R. Hanson, who was
at the time Marshal of Mt. Olivet, and as an officer had

arrested some of the regulators for disorderly conduct about a month ago. Dayton had a difficulty with William Claypole, who is believed to be a regulator, about a hog. It is said Claypole last Saturday, while drunk at Mt. Olivet, said, "We are going to settle with Dayton to-night, and he will never make another settlement." Claypole, Henry Rankine and Alfred Murray have been arrested on suspicion. They are now in jail at Mt. Olivet. Dayton was about 40 years old and is in good circumstances. He leaves a wife and six children. There is a good deal of excitement over the affair in Robertson.

As I prepared to leave my grandpas, I stood up, took off my hat, and had a few words with them. Then replacing my hat on my head, I snapped my heels together, as I had for Alex. I gave these old soldiers a snappy salute. It was getting dark, and I needed to be on my way.

I learned that the Hamm and Dayton families were some of the earliest settlers in Kentucky. They go back to about 1780. For reference, Daniel Boone founded Boonesborough, Kentucky, in 1775.

Those were two graves I was successful in finding. I have lots of graves to locate before I'm through on this Earth, including Jacob Hamm, and Henry Banta, who both fought in the American Revolution before coming to Kentucky from Virginia. They descend from my grandfather, Charles Henry Hamm, and his wife, my grandmother, Rosa Scott Hamm.

I hope you enjoyed my story. Now git on outta here. Go on now, git! Your prospects of working yourself into my mind right now ain't too promising, but I still love ya.

Take the
Right Road

Loving one another is a better way,
even if you disagree.

John Robert Dayton, Proud Patriot

"You don't choose your family.
They are God's gift to you as you are to them."
~Desmond Tutu

Never give advice to those who don't ask, and be selective of those who do.

I told my story of finding my great-great-grandfather, John Robert Dayton's grave and shared that he fought for the Union in the Civil War, as well as that he was murdered by regulators on 27 July 1878, in Mount Olivet, Kentucky.

Since the writing of his story, I have learned more. After returning from the war in 1865, his wife, Caroline Jane Millikin Dayton, bore him a daughter. What speaks volumes to me is he named her "America."

John Robert was a proud patriot and surely proud of his service. His daughter's name represents that.

Though he possibly didn't know it, on the day of his death, Caroline was two months pregnant. She gave birth to a son on 6 February 1879 and named him John Robert Dayton, Jr., in honor of his father. That is my great-grandfather.

It is so special to learn more than just the names of our ancestors. When we start learning their stories and stand before their graves, they come alive in our hearts.

I can't wait for my next journey into the past.

For now, I'm trying to give Thelma, the doe matriarch of the mountain, a belly rub, and she wants my undivided attention. So stop distractin' me.

We'll talk later, I'm sure.

It's Not Over
'Til It's over

Your golden years are before you.
Embrace them.
Make the best of them.
Continue to dream.

MAKE A MEMORY

"Time isn't the main thing.
It's the only thing."
~Miles Davis

Look here, nobody ever laid dying and wished they had made more money.

Hard work, making your own way, serving others, and providing for your families are certainly important, but some things are of far greater value.

I shared the moment captured in the picture below with my twelve-year-old cookie bandit, Lillie, at a 5K race Saturday morning. Such moments are priceless. By the way, Lillie came in first in the age group fourteen and under.

On another day, I spent time with my nine-year-old grandson, Lucas, who had just one thing to say as he guarded the lacrosse net, "Not today, Sparky, not today!"

Guess what? I would have missed that if I hadn't made time to go to his game. I could have never gotten that time back.

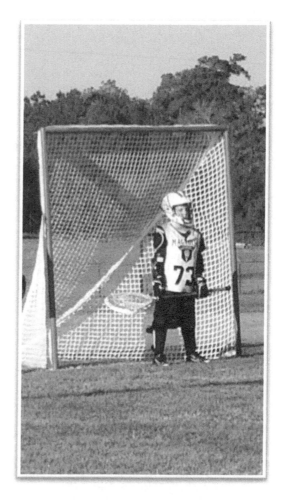

Okay, enough of the sappy old grandpa. Don't be thinking I'm going soft. Git on outta here and go find a child you love and give them a hug. Make a memory.

Don't Use a
Ten-Dollar Word

If you have something to say or write, use plain talk.
Simplicity is wonderfully profound.

THE EXISTENCE OF SOMETHING

"By replacing fear of the unknown with curiosity,
we open ourselves to an infinite stream of possibility."
~Alan Watts

The existence of something stands as evidence of something capable of bringing it into existence. If you don't grasp the significance of this simple, universal truth, you'll never understand anything—even if you're one of the smart people.

Don't Repeat History

We can learn from our own personal history.
It helps make for a more promising future.

LEAVING THE NEST

"Feeling sad to leave doesn't mean you shouldn't go."
~ Unknown

Becoming an adult means growing up, leaving the nest, and taking responsibility for yourself.

If you still depend on others to take care of you, whether it's your mama or the government, you're still a child. I don't care how old you are.

I like independence.

I pondered that very thought as the bad storms whipped through Round Mountain this weekend.

All I could do was rock, think, and have a snort—or two.

Every critter was laying low. They're wise like that, and I pay attention to their habits. That's the time to go home, for shelter as they do. Otherwise, you have to fend for yourself. There's no excuse to do otherwise.

I was in a storm myself. Not one blowing inside me, but out.

A Texas Blue Norther blew in down here a week or two ago. Well, I got a good fire going in the cabin and invited all the critters inside. Thangs went purdy good 'til they went to watching movies.

In one, a young woman needed a liver transplant, and some Marine came out of the blue and donated his to save her life. The operations went well; those two got to sparkin' up and ended up getting hitched. The critters loved it.

The next day, another movie showed that same woman scoping out another man. For some reason, Spuds, leader of the wild hog clan, got really upset about it and started calling her bad names. This violated the Round Mountain Critter Code of Conduct, so Thelma stepped in and got into it with Spuds. Other than that, everthang went well.

Okay, I gotta scram. The cabin is a mess, and I got stuff to do.

That's Only
the Half of It

Wisdom will always be a casualty of unrestrained behavior.

THANK GOD FOR DAYS THAT TEST YOUR METTLE

"We must accept finite disappointment
but never lose infinite hope."
~Martin Luther King

Life is an amazing adventure.

We awaken each morning to another day that will be unique in its own special way.

No day will be perfect. We know that.

Having a calm spirit and being content depends on how you choose to look at things.

One day, I was miserable in body. It was thirty-four degrees, foggy, with misty rain, and the wind was blowing about twenty-five miles an hour.

I WAS WET AND FREEZING MY BUTT OFF. HOWEVER, IT WAS A SPECIAL DAY.

Inwardly, I knew the imperfections of that day were making a memory. So, deep down inside, I was grinning, just doing my job.

That day provided me a story to tell that will make me and others laugh.

And I'll make it a good story!

I thank God for life and special days that test your mettle.

It's in Your Hands

Life is neutral.
We choose who we become.

"DID YOU THANK HIM FOR THE WORK?"

"The best way to appreciate your job
is to imagine yourself without one."
~ Oscar Wilde

When I was ten years old, and the summer break began, I was determined to get a job and make some money.

There was a fruit farm about two miles from where I lived, so I walked cross country through fields and woods, met the owner, and asked him if he needed any help.

HE HIRED ME, AND I WENT TO WORK PICKING STRAWBERRIES FOR FIFTY CENTS AN HOUR. HE PAID ME IN FIFTY-CENT PIECES, SO AT THE END OF THE DAY, I WALKED BACK HOME WITH EIGHT HALF DOLLARS IN MY POCKET.

I felt rich.

I felt proud.

When I saw my daddy and told him, he looked at me firmly and asked me a question I have never forgotten, "Did you thank him for the work?"

I told him that I did not remember saying so, and he then said something else I have never forgotten, "If a man gives you a job, thank him every day. Make him a good hand."

The next day, when I got my pay, and it was time to go home, I told my boss, "Thanks for the work." I'll never forget the look on his face when I told him that.

Daddy was born in 1918 and came of age during the depression of the 1930s. Living far out in the country, it was nearly impossible for anyone to find gainful employment. The family was very poor, living on what grew in the garden, what Grandma canned, and wild game, for the most part. Fried rabbit, and squirrels, or fish caught in the creek most often graced the dinner table.

At that time, there weren't government programs to "help" such people. However, from those times came what we now think of as the "Greatest Generation."

Daddy was drafted into the Army during World War II and did not really have a good-paying, permanent job until 1945.

TO THAT GENERATION, A JOB WAS A SACRED TRUST TO BE TREASURED AND FOR WHICH TO BE THANKFUL.

He was a hardworking man who would not think of betraying the confidence of his employer by not giving him a hard day's work.

To this day, I never have forgotten the words of my father.

Every time a client gives us a project to do, without fail, I will tell him, "Thanks for the work." I then feel obligated to work hard and give them my very best. I owe it to them, I owe it to myself, I owe it to the men who work for me, and I owe it to my daddy.

How things have changed.

So often, today, people think a job is a "right," something owed to them. They feel no obligation to be thankful or be a "good hand."

How sad.

A strong work ethic seems like something from another time. But, thanks to my daddy, I am a man from another time.

Daddy died in 1990.

I still think of him, miss him, and have not, and will never forget that day he asked me, "Did you thank him for the work?"

Yes sir, I did.

Whenever You Have the Chance

Never pass up an opportunity to give
honor to whom honor is due.
It will touch the hearts of both of you.

RUMINATIONS OF AN
OLD WORK HORSE

"A single leaf working alone provides no shade."
~ Chuck Page

Let me throw this at you: how would you define a job?

I've found in my musing that the word is not defined, as is true of life, beyond manifestations.

Really, a job is born out of the needs of others. Someone needs help and is willing to give something of value—usually money—to someone who will provide the service. It exists only on the *level of need*. The manifestations of the job begin when it is filled.

A job is a sacred trust between two people. One pledges an agreed amount of compensation, and one pledges to provide service of equal value. The two are bound together by honor, integrity, and trust, concepts that elevate us to our best self: spirit.

Before I retired, a frequent subject of my posts was about the dignity of work. I spoke of the joy and sense of satisfaction that we should feel about doing our job well.

I define work as service to our fellow man.

AS I TOLD YOU, I GOT MY FIRST JOB WHEN I WAS TEN YEARS OLD, PICKING STRAWBERRIES. I WORKED HARD UNTIL I WAS SEVENTY-FOUR YEARS OLD. THEN, OVERNIGHT, NOT ONE PERSON IN THE WORLD DEPENDED ON ME FOR ANYTHING.

This was quite an adjustment for me.

For the first few months, it was kind of nice to have nothing to do; I have to admit. I stayed up later and slept later. I read some great books. I gave more belly rubs to my critters.

Then feelings of being old and useless started creeping into my mind. I needed a reason to live, or what was the point? Old demons that have followed me around since I was a young man started whispering to me. I couldn't have that.

Now, I'm happy to announce that I'm back in the saddle, so to speak, having thrown myself into marketing for my family locating business.

I'm doing mailouts to businesses that might need our services and am under absolutely no pressure from anyone to do anything if I don't feel like it.

My time is still my own.

Even though it is—I'm working like a man obsessed. This has rekindled my spark for life.

I Swear on My Hat This Works

If you want to be happy, first learn to laugh at yourself.

The Life of an Oil Field Dog

"You keep me safe, and I'll keep you wild."
- Unknown

He seemed to come from nowhere.

One day he just appeared.

No one knew who he was, his name, or where he came from.

One thing was obvious.

His life had taken what must have seemed like a horrible turn for the worst, and now, lost and alone, he found his way to the oil field.

Immediately he found the love of all who worked in the field, and he returned it in spades.

He was named Solo Vivo because it means: "He came alone."

Solo Vivo, pictured below, now gets all the food he wants, has shelter, runs free, and gives and receives love from all he meets. From what must have seemed the depths of despair for a dog came the best of times for him. The life of an oil field dog is a good one.

Sometimes in life, things happen that seem devastating at the time, but often what follows turns out to be the best thing that ever happened to you.

Let Solo Vivo inspire you to remember that when you need it.

A Last Ponderin'
Before You Git

I suppose it is understandable that when we get older, we will reflect back over our lives.

It's a good thing.

We can learn from our own personal history, which helps make for a more promising future.

We all do dumb stuff.

We all make mistakes.

We all go stupid.

We all know times when we should have done one thing but did the other.

We say things we shouldn't have said and don't say things we should have.

What is important is that we learn to forgive ourselves.

We have to let things go and not beat ourselves up over our failures.

We must learn from our mistakes, move on, and be a better person.

THE KEYS TO FUTURE VICTORIES WILL BE FOUND IN YOUR PAST DEFEATS.

Do I have regrets as I look back over my life?

NO, I don't.

Lessons learned?

Oh yeah. Lots of 'em.

Ponder on it, pilgrims.

Oh, and don't ever forget, I love ya all.

Thanks for reading my book.

I'm glad you horsed me into it, after all.

Now, shucks, I've written a book. Go figure.

ABOUT THE AUTHOR

"Texan to the bone" Charles Hamm is a veteran Marine sergeant and a retired successful businessman and entrepreneur. He holds a BA degree from David Lipscomb University in Classical Greek and Hebrew and is a passionate student of ancient history.

Charles is well-known on LinkedIn for sharing his thoughts about life and lessons learned from seventy-five years of navigating the twists, turns, and ups and downs of life's often perilous roads we all travel.

He and his wife Kathy, married 54 years, have three children and seven grandchildren. They reside in Magnolia, Texas, where they are enjoying their golden years.

To get in touch with Charles and learn more about his latest creative endeavors, please visit: CharlesHamm.com.

Made in the USA
Coppell, TX
06 April 2022

76121699R00134